aircraft illustrated

ANNUAL 1987

COMPETITION COUPON 1987

£6.00

Cover:
A310-221 Airbus HB-IPE of Swissair on finals to land at Heathrow. *Peter R. March*

Previous page:
A No 74 'Tiger' Squadron Lightning T5 XV329 at low level off the Singapore coast. *Peter R. March*

Below:
American and British Harriers in flight. The US Marine Corps ordered the first of 120 AV-8As in 1971. It is seen here in company with a RAF GR1 and T2. *Peter R. March*

aircraft illustrated
ANNUAL 1987

Edited by PETER R. MARCH

LONDON

IAN ALLAN LTD

A No 829 Squadron Wasp is guided on to the tiny deck of a frigate. *Rolls-Royce*

First published 1986

ISBN 0 7110 1632 1

Published by Ian Allan Ltd, Shepperton, Surrey; and printed by Ian Allan Printing Ltd at their works at Coombelands in Runnymede, England

Contents

Paul Jackson

The Mirage in Middle Age

Great oak trees grow from little acorns — but in the world of aviation, long and successful production runs stem from small contracts. Thus, it was an almost unbelievable 30 years ago that France's air force placed an inititial order for a trials batch of just 10 examples of a promising design known as the Dassault Mirage III. In 1985, when the assembly lines at Bordeaux at last fell silent, 1,411 of the first-generation Mirage had been supplied to 21 countries, establishing France as a world-class exporter of potent military aircraft. As in the case of many a classic warplane, far-sightedness and innovation were the twin keys to outstanding performance, and employed in generous measure by Dassault they produced an aircraft which l'Armée de l'Air could not refuse.

That was not to say that the Mirage III was what the air force had asked for when it issued a specification for a new fighter in 1953. Basing its requirements on what appeared to be the lessons of Sabre v MiG-15 combat in Korea, France asked for a small interceptor with such a high climb rate and ceiling that only a combination of turbojet and liquid-fuelled rocket motor could meet the demands. Dassault's MD550 Mystère Delta, first flown at Melun-Villaroche, south of Paris, on 25 June 1955 was one submission, but low power from its two Armstrong-Siddeley Vipers resulted in it having a disappointing performance.

Above:
First of the many. The diminutive MD550 was first flown in 1955. *AG Photo Press Aero*

Below:
Clearly well on the way to the well known 'Mirage shape', the Mirage III-001 was flown in November 1956.
AG Photo Press Aero

Soon renamed 'Mirage I', the MD550 was impractically small for an all-weather interceptor. However, the effort in producing it was not wasted, for it had been a valuable testbed for the still novel delta configuration. The basic shape was right for high-speed flight; all that was needed was an airframe big enough to carry radar, all-weather avionics and hard-hitting armament. In the stillborn Mirage II, to have been powered by a pair of Turbomeca Gabizo turbojets, a far more practical aeroplane began to emerge on the drawing boards. When this design was refined with the results of US researches into the aerodynamic 'Area Rule', British discoveries with the speed record-breaking Fairey FD2, and a single new Atar turbojet from SNECMA, the result was the Mirage III.

Airborne for the first time in the hands of Roland Glavany on 17 November 1956, the Mirage III No 001 began well and carried on even better. During the 10th flight, on 30 January 1957, the 3,300lb (1,500kg) thrust SEPR 66 rocket was fitted in the lower fuselage for the first time and boosted speed to Mach 1.52 in conjunction with the 9,920lb (4,500kg) from

Above:
The prototype Mirage IIIE No 01 displayed new features including a lengthened fuselage. *Marcel Dassault*

Below:
Mirage IIIA No 05 first flown on 10 May 1959 was almost identical to the initial production series.
AG Photo Press Aero

the Atar 101G-1. The next step forward was to fit manually-operated half-cone centrebodies in the air intakes to enable the pilot to focus the shock wave at the optimum position for engine efficiency. An improvement in high speed thrust of no less than 20% was the result — clearly demonstrated when the aircraft reached Mach 1.80 on 17 April 1958.

The results of the first production order now began to make themselves felt in the evolution of a fighting aeroplane from a research vehicle. Mirage IIIA was the designation of the 10 development aircraft, the first of which (IIIA-01) flew on 12 May 1958 — again with Glavany at the controls. It was No 01 which, on 24 October 1958, became the first French aircraft to fly at Mach 2.0 without rocket assistance, thereby beating the English Electric Lightning to that speed by one month. The time margin was narrow, but significant, for Britain had not suffered a hiatus in military aircraft development because of German occupation during World War 2. France had been forced to start almost from scratch with jet aircraft research in 1945, and had now undeniably caught up with Europe's leader.

Remaining Mirage IIIAs appeared during 1959, each concentrating on a particular aspect of the programme: radar, engine, avionics, etc. Not that there was now any doubt about the Mirage III's future following the placing of an order for 100 on 5 August 1958 — less than three months after IIIA-01 had flown. Initial production was of the Mirage IIIC which was delivered to the famous 'Cigognes' fighter squadron (Escadron de Chasse 1/2 at Dijon) from 10 July 1961 onwards. Appropriately, the 'C' type suffix reflected 'Chasse', the French word for fighter, although the original concept of a pure interceptor had changed after the aircraft's potential had been recognised during development. Henceforth, the Mirage III was promoted as a multi-role aircraft — and very successfully, as it turned out.

In total, 95 Mirage IIICs were delivered to l'Armée de l'Air, and it was not until May 1985 that the last of these assigned to defence of home airspace was withdrawn from front-line service. Even so, one further unit (Escadron de Chasse 'Vexin') is based in the former French colony of Djibouti, East Africa, as a deterrent to threatened Somali aggression. Also still performing a useful role are the early Mirage IIIB two-seat trainers and their later counterparts,

Below:
A two-seat Mirage IIIB trainer landing at Bordeaux-Merignac. *Andrew March*

Bottom:
The last Mirage IIICs assigned to home defence were at Creil with EC2/10 'Seine', which disbanded in 1985.
Peter R. March

Above:
Armed with a pair of Sidewinders, a Swiss Mirage IIIS gets airborne with JATO assistance. *Swiss Air Force*

the IIIBE. France bought 20 IIIBEs as parallels to the IIIE ground attack and tactical strike model of the Mirage, identifiable by its longer fuselage and forward-raked undercarriage legs (to accommodate an AN52 nuclear weapon on the centreline pylon). Including three prototypes — flown from 5 April 1961 onwards — 192 Mirage IIIEs were delivered between 1964 and 1973, survivors remaining in service with five squadrons in the mid-1980s. They now rarely — if ever — use the rocket booster, its location instead accommodating additional fuel.

Replacement of the IIIE's Thomson-CSF Cyrano radar by a camera nose, produced the tactical reconnaissance Mirage IIIR, a prototype flying for the first time on 31 October 1961. Fifty, plus a further 20 IIIRDs with Doppler navigation equipment, were built between 1963 and 1969 for three squadrons of the 33rd Recce Wing at Strasbourg. Now, two squadrons have converted to Mirage F1CR-200s, leaving just Escadron de Reconnaissance 3/33 'Moselle' with Mirage IIIRDs. Finally, in 1972, l'Armée de l'Air received a windfall in the form of 50 Mirage 5Fs previously ordered by Israel as Mirage 5Js, but embargoed after the 1967 Arab-Israeli war. A simplified Mirage IIIE, lacking radar and other all-weather avionics, the 5F was issued to two French squadrons, which still employ it for ground attack missions. A further eight Mirage 5Fs were supplied in 1983-85 to replace a similar number transferred to Chile in a rush transaction during 1979.

French aircraft represent less than half the Mirage III/5 story. Tailored to meet individual customer requirements, dozens of different models of the popular delta have been sold as far afield as Australia and participated in combat against a variety of opponents. Israel, an early customer for 72 Mirage IIICJs (similar to the basic IIIC) first took the aircraft into battle on 20 August 1963 when two Syrian MiG-17s were destroyed. Mirages confirmed their superiority in other skirmishes before inflicting terrible losses upon their Arab neighbours' air forces on 5 June 1967. In the opening hours of the Six Day War, Mirages played a major part in the air attacks which destroyed 300 Egyptian aircraft on the ground before turning their attention, equally successfully, to Jordan and Syria. Time

Top:
The RAAF operated Mirage IIIOs in the air defence role until 1986. *Peter R. March*

Centre:
The light-weight, ground-attack Mirage 5 has been widely adopted. This Belgian Air Force Mirage VBA has under-wing fuel tanks. *Peter R. March*

Above:
A Venezuelan Air Force Mirage 5 with reduced avionics, being optimised for attack missions. *Dassault-Breguet*

employed in designing the Mirage for ease of turn-round servicing proved well spent as the aircraft took off for the front again a mere seven minutes after landing, instead of the average 20 expected from other fighters. Mirages flew 12 sorties in a day, to the disbelief of adversaries who were convinced that Israel had been given additional combat aircraft by other countries.

Such was Israel's faith in the Mirage that when the 50 further aircraft were embargoed, an unlicensed copy was produced by IAI as the Nesher and later fitted with a General Electric J79 engine and new avionics to become the Kfir. Neshers were used in the attack role for the 1973 war before being sold to Argentina under the name Dagger and suffering at the hands of Royal Navy Sea Harriers in the Falklands War. Two Argentine Mirage IIIEAs were also lost in combat, and to make good the attrition, 19 of the original battle-hardened Mirage IIICJs were bought from Israel in 1982. Less well remembered are the conflicts of December 1971 in which Pakistani Mirage IIIEPs claimed eight Indian aircraft in air combat (and two on the ground) with no loss to themselves.

Weaponry used by the various Mirage variants is as diverse as it is impressive. In air-to-air roles, the aircraft will carry a medium-range MATRA R530 missile on the centreline (semi-active radar or infra-red homing) and a pair of close-in American AIM-9 Sidewinders or MATRA R550 Magics (both IR) beneath the wings. Two internal DEFA 552 30mm cannon, with 125 rounds each, may be used against air and ground targets. Mirage IIIs have five weapon attachment points and Mirage 5s, seven, allowing carriage of up to 8,820lb (4,000kg) of ordnance or additional fuel. Typically, this might include general purpose or Durandal anti-runway bombs; 68mm or 100mm rocket pods; and combined fuel and rocket pods. Some Mirages supplied to Pakistan have Aérospatiale AM39 Exocet anti-ship missiles and appropriate Thomson-CSF Agave air-to-surface radar in the nose.

Only Israel has disposed of its Mirage IIIs, the other operators continuing to find useful employment for the ageing, but still very capable, fighter-bomber. Abu Dhabi, Argentina, Australia, Belgium, Brazil, Chile, Colombia, Egypt, Gabon, Lebanon, Libya, Pakistan, Peru, South Africa, Spain, Switzerland, Venezuela and Zaire are current operators (although Saudi Arabia is, strictly speaking, another purchaser, having paid for some directly transferred to Egypt). Those for Chile are designated Mirage 50 to reflect their fitment with an uprated Atar 9K-50 engine in place of the Atar 9C of most production Mirages.

Some users have opted for update programmes to keep their Mirages effective for a further tour of service, but none has yet gone as far as ordering the Mirage 3NG. A demonstrator for this 'Nouvelle Génération' Mirage III flew on 21 December 1982, featuring a fly-by-wire control system, inertial navigation and other advanced avionics from the Mirage 2000. The canard foreplanes included in the Mirage 3NG

Below:
This Mirage IIIEBR is known in Brazil as the F-103E, serving with 1 Grupo de Difesa Aerea at Anapolis. *AG Photo Press Aero*

Bottom:
One of the less well-known Mirage users is Zaire, represented here by a Mirage 5DM of No 211 Squadron at Kamina. *Dassault-Breguet*

Top:
Mirage IIIEs like this example will continue in service with the French Air Force, principally for ground attack duties. *Peter R. March*

Above:
Last of the line. The Mirage 3NG appeared at the 1983 Paris Air Show, showing its up-dated configuration.
AG Photo Press Aero

design, and also seen on the Kfir, improve manoeuvrability and short field performance. They will appear in the future on Mirage IIIs being refurbished by Switzerland and South Africa.

Whilst the Mirage 3NG appears to have come too late to make a significant impression on the combat aircraft market, there is no denying the longevity of the basic Mirage III/5/50 series. Thirty years is a very long time in the fast moving world of the warplane, yet for two-thirds of that period, a queue of new customers was to be found outside Dassault's door, convinced that the first generation Mirage was the right aircraft for them. (The queue is still there — but it is now for Mirage F1s and Mirage 2000s.) Other 1950s fighters may have their retirement dates already pencilled-in on the calendar; the remarkable Mirage has only just admitted to being middle-aged.

Derek James

Schneider Losers

We all love a winner. But this is a story about losers, for without them there cannot be winners. Everyone knows the winner. But it's the quality of the losers which makes the contest worth winning and which often makes a major contribution to advancement in their particular field.

In 1931, the Supermarine S6B floatplane not only won the Schneider Trophy for Great Britain for all time but also a permanent niche for itself in aviation's hall of fame. Almost forgotten is the first of the three consecutive victories in these contests which enabled Britain to be the perpetual holder of this magnificent trophy. It was nearly 60 years ago, on 26 September 1927 that Flt Lt S. N. Webster, flying a blue and silver Supermarine S5, beat off the challenge of three scarlet Italian Macchi M52 racing floatplanes to win the 10th Schneider Contest in Venice at an average speed of 281.655mph.

Who were the losers in all of the other 11 contests? What were those aircraft which failed to come to the start line or, indeed, never got off the drawing board, between 1913 and 1931, the years in which the first and last Schneider Contests were flown?

To begin at the beginning. In 1910 Jacques Schneider, the son of a wealthy French industrialist, had a dream. It was that as 70% of the earth's surface is covered by water, the seaplane should be developed as a universal form of transport, providing a communications system linking most parts of the world. In December 1912, in an effort to encourage and speed the development of passenger-carrying seaplanes, Schneider announced that he was to establish a special contest for this type of aeroplane. He would award a trophy and provide £1,000 annually for the initial three contests, the first of which was held at Monaco on 16 April 1913. Sadly, neither the trophy, the money nor the contests motivated designers to create commercial seaplanes. Nevertheless there were, for Britain at least, some splendid dividends from the contests as a return for the heavy investment in terms of time, money, effort and lives.

We know the names of many of the winning aircraft or their designers and pilots. Britain's Supermarine S6B, designed by Reginald J. Mitchell and flown by Flt Lt John Boothman; the US-built Curtiss R3C-2 and Lt James Doolittle, the pilot; Major Mario de Bernardi and his Macchi M39. These were winners. On the other hand there was Edouard de Nieport — who changed his name to Nieuport because his family regarded his aviation fame as outrageous notoriety — and there were Roger Robert of the French Bernard company, Alessandro Marchetti and Giovanni Pegna of Italy, Harry Folland of Gloster, Col A. W. Bristow and W. George Carter of Short, and Cdr J. Hunsaker of the US Navy Bureau of Aeronautics — all were losers. At least their designs, when turned into hardware, were among the 70 aircraft which were withdrawn from the lists of potential contest entrants. Some crashed on test, some never got off the water, some simply

Below:
What it was all about, La Coupe d'Aviation Maritime Jacques Schneider.

broke down. To these can be added at least 15 projects, and there may have been more, which existed only on paper. Let's look at some of the more interesting of them.

Roland Garros' 1913 Morane-Saulnier Hydro-monoplane was just about the minimum racing floatplane: simply a square-section wooden fabric-covered fuselage, a pair of wood and fabric wings without ailerons, no fin nor tailplane, only a small rudder and elevator, all mounted on a pair of floats and hauled along at a hopeful 75mph by the almost inevitable 80hp Gnome rotary engine. It was beaten into second place by the more efficient Deperdussin monoplane, to become the first loser in the contest by only 3mph. In 1914 the Sopwith Tabloid's winning margin over the second-placed Swiss FBA flying boat was more convincing, for about 1hr 24min separated them! True, poor Henri Burri, the Swiss pilot, had to alight three-quarters of the way through the contest to refuel; but he was an also-ran in the history books.

A contest rule was that the country winning the trophy should host and organise the following year's event. Thus, Bournemouth was the venue for the 1919 contest, dubbed 'the fiasco in the fog' due to the total lack of any

Above:
This unidentified man gives scale to the little Morane-Saulnier Hydro-monoplane, one of the losers at Monaco in 1913. *Musée de l'Air*

organisation on the part of the Royal Aero Club. The Fairey III, flown by Vincent Nicholl got airborne but having nearly hit both the mast of a turning point marker boat and another aircraft in the fog, he gave up and returned to Bournemouth. Both Harry Hawker in the Sopwith Schneider and Basil Hobbs in Supermarine's Sea Lion, did an encore with Hobbs going one better — or worse — by ramming something in the water as he attempted to take off, which holed the hull and sank the Sea Lion. The Spad-Herbemont S20 bis biplane floatplane never made it to the start line, even though its pilot, the renowned Sadi Lecointe, had sawn some two feet off the tip of each top wing as a 'go-faster' modification. One of its floats sprang a leak and could not be repaired sufficiently quickly to meet a constantly changing start time.

The winning Italian Savoia S13 was subsequently disqualified for flying an incorrect course, but a grace-and-favour decision by the Fédération Aéronautique Internationale

allowed Italy to host the 1920 Contest — which it won because there were no other entrants, and duly repeated this exercise for the same reason in 1921! Although about 18 aircraft were withdrawn from that year's contest, two Macchi M7s and an M19 flying boat managed to get into the air, the M19 becoming the only aircraft in the history of the contests to have a two-man crew when pilot Arturo Zanetti took along his mechanic named Pedetti. Its 650hp Fiat A14 12-cylinder engine set a record too; this 57-litre engine was the largest to take part in any Schneider event. No wonder it broke its crankshaft out on the course, caught fire and completely burnt out down to the waterline.

Top:
A fast-taxying Nieuport. Three of this type were withdrawn in 1913 because of damage or total loss. *Musée de l'Air*

Above:
Sadi Lecointe's Spad-Herbemont S20 bis at Bournemouth in 1919, with the starboard float taking water after damage. *Flight*

Two interesting Italian flying boats among those withdrawn were the twin-boom pusher-engined Macchi M12 and the pretty little Savoia S21 in which the upper wing was 33% shorter in span than the lower one. Victories in the 1920 and 1921 contests put Italy well on the road to becoming the permanent owner of the trophy but the winner which sprang a few surprises at Naples in 1922 was the old Supermarine Sea Lion flown by Henri Biard. France's CAMS36, a dainty little biplane flying boat, capsized during preliminary trials while the equally appealing Savoia S51 sesquiplane flying boat entrant, which also capsized during mooring-out trials, suffered problems during the contest when the propeller laminations began to part after their soaking. This frustrated the attempts of Alessandro Passaleva, the pilot, to overtake Biard in the Sea Lion II.

This great victory gave Britain the privilege of hosting the 1923 contest. Then the cry went up 'the Yanks are coming'. And come they did, with typical US efficiency and thoroughness, bringing four aircraft and a large team of pilots and mechanics. They arrived a month before the contest to acclimatise themselves and to practice their flying techniques over the Solent.

Britain's Blackburn Pellet flying boat had had a chequered career by the time it got to Fairey Aviation's hangars at Hamble. It had capsized almost immediately after being launched into the River Humber at Brough, and then, when it

came south, it required hurried overnight modifications in Sammy Saunders' hangar at Cowes where a larger radiator was fitted. When R. W. Kenworthy attempted an early morning take-off, some fool in a rowing boat pulled slowly across his path. He rammed open the throttle of the Napier Lion engine and hauled back on the control column, but the Pellet began to porpoise, leaping into the air and then dropping back into the sea. When it managed to get airborne it was in a semi-stalled attitude, and then one wing tip touched the water. The Pellet turned over and dived below the surface. It was 61 seconds by the timekeeper's watch before Kenworthy's head bobbed to the surface and he was rescued.

The US had its problems too. The big Wright NW-2 floatplane suffered engine troubles and only one practice run with the specially-tuned engine was attempted. However, it blew up 20 minutes after take-off and the NW-2 was written off in the subsequent crash. A backfire wrecked the engine inertial starting system of the Naval Aircraft Factory's TR-3 floatplane and, as it could not be hand swung, it was withdrawn from the list of starters. Of five French aircraft chosen to cross the Channel to Cowes, only one, the CAMS38 pusher biplane flying boat participated, but it retired after two laps leaving two US Curtiss CR-3s to take first and second places ahead of the updated Supermarine Sea Lion III.

The Baltimore 1924 Schneider Contest was unique — it never happened. In Britain the Supermarine Sea Urchin flying boat project did not progress beyond the planning stage and the Gloster II floatplane crashed at Felixstowe during early flight testing. Other projects from Italy, France and Germany failed to become hardware and the US Wright F2W2 also crashed on test. The United States had only to fly a Curtiss CR3 leisurely around the course to claim the trophy but, in a most sporting gesture, it declared the contest cancelled for that year.

Baltimore 1925 saw the sole appearance of cantilever monoplanes among the entries. They were Britain's Supermarine S4 floatplane with a 700hp Napier Lion engine and Italy's Macchi M33 flying boat powered by a second-hand 430hp Curtiss D-12A engine bought from the US. Reg Mitchell's S4 was a quantum leap forward into the unknown and, in pre-race practice flying, it plunged into Chesapeake Bay after Biard had experienced either wing flutter or possibly aileron reversal. Italy's M33 was

Above:
This flying view of the unfortunate Macchi M19 shows the Warren girder-type wing struts and the 57-litre Fiat A14 engine. *Aeronautica Macchi*

Right:
The unusually configured Savoia S21 flying boat was removed from the 1921 contest list of entrants when its pilot, Sgt Guido Jannello, fell ill.

Below right:
In this photo of the Blackburn Pellet's fateful take-off in 1923, the hull is just clear of the water and the nose is coming up. A split second later it hit the surface, rolled over and sank. *Hawker Siddeley Aviation*

simply not fast enough to contain either the blistering speed of Doolittle and his Curtiss R3C-2 floatplane or the guile of Hubert Broad in the Gloster III biplane which toddled home in second place.

The following year the United States, with two consecutive victories under its belt, had only to win at home at the Hampton Roads, Norfolk, Virginia, venue to give the Schneider Trophy a permanent home in the New World. Unfortunately for Britain two private venture projects were abandoned — as were two from Macchi and one from Dornier — and the Supermarine S5 and Gloster IV floatplanes lacked their new Napier Lion VII engines when it became time for them to be on the ship to Norfolk. But the strong US position and the lack of British competition only served to spur on Benito Mussolini, the Italian dictator, who decided to show the world that Fascism could do more than make his country's trains run on time. He decreed that Italy must win the 1926 Contest at all costs — met by the Government; and that's just what the scarlet Macchi M39s did at an average speed of 246.496mph. A starter in this contest was the US Navy's Curtiss F6C-3 Hawk, which, as its designation implies, was a fighter-on-floats and, with only 60% of the power of the Macchi floatplanes, was last across the finishing line averaging 110mph less than the Italians.

Italy's victory added new life to the contest series and once again opened up the possibilities of advancing Europe's knowledge of high speed flight and the means to achieve it. By 1927 it was clear that Britain had at last perceived the need to be fully prepared for the event in Venice. Thus, through a decision made two years earlier, Gloster, Shorts and Supermarine had produced no less than seven aircraft; added to these was the formation of an RAF High Speed Flight at Felixstowe.

This contest in Venice was, in reality, the beginning of the end of the Schneider series for, as described earlier, the Supermarine S5 averaged 281.6mph to win handsomely with another S5 coming in second place only 8mph slower. But before this British victory there were many disappointments too for Britain, as well as for France, Italy and the United States. France could not raise a team, while the Short-Bristow Crusader — nicknamed *Curious Ada* by the High Speed Flight pilots, and unusual in that it had a 960hp Bristol Mercury radial engine — was the victim of crossed aileron control cables during flight trials in Venice. On take-off it started to roll to starboard but when Flg Off H. M. Schofield applied what he believed to be corrective aileron, it rolled over completely, broke in two and sank. Happily the

pilot was rescued. The handsome Gloster IV biplane was lapping steadily at around 275mph in the contest but retired in the sixth when its Lion engine appeared to falter. Back in the hangar when the propeller was removed it was discovered that the propeller shaft was cracked threequarters around its diameter. Across the Atlantic the private venture Kirkham-Williams floatplane lacked both the performance to be a credible contender and the financial backing to change this situation; thus it was withdrawn. Italy, defending the trophy, produced three Macchi 52s which were very fast in practice; in the contest, however, their Fiat AS3 engines failed one by one and all retired.

Without doubt, from the aircraft enthusiasts' point of view, the 1929 Schneider Contest at Calshot was the most interesting, if only because it produced a crop of Italian aeroplanes which richly deserved the title 'the good, the bad, the ugly — and the impossible'. But more of these later.

Three projects, one from Dornier plus Italy's highly unconventional Pegna Pc5 tandem-engined and Pc6 retractable planing bottom projects were not built. Time and money again ran out for the US private venture Williams Mercury which, even with an enormous 1,250hp Packard X-2772 24-cylinder 'X' engine, could not be coaxed off the water for more than a hundred yards or so. In France the Bernard company produced the HV40 and HV42 monoplanes with an 800hp Gnome-Rhone Mistral radial and a 1,000hp Hispano Suiza Special in-line engine respectively, while Nieuport-Delage built the ND450, a handsome similarly-configured design but with the more powerful 1,680hp Hispano Suiza 18R engine. None of them was ready for the contest and France withdrew.

There was much disappointment in the Gloster camp when, having produced two examples of the Gloster VI floatplane, dubbed the *Golden Arrow* and described in the daily and technical press as 'the most beautiful aeroplane ever built', their 1,320hp Napier Lion VIID engines could not be kept running at full throttle in the air, particularly when turning. The bitter pill of withdrawal was sweetened a little on the day after the contest when a new Absolute Speed Record of 336.30mph was established.

Of the quartet of Italian designs only one — the 'good' Macchi M67 with a 1,800hp Isotta-Fraschini engine — became a contestant. However, both examples experienced engine-associated problems and were forced to alight out on the course. The 'ugly' Fiat C29 earned

Below:
The engine of the US Navy Wright NW-2, seen here at Cowes in 1923, blew up on its first practice flight.

Above right:
One of France's two Latham L1 flying boats. Neither managed to get to the starting line at Cowes in 1923.

Right:
About to be launched at Woolston in 1925, the ill-fated Supermarine S4 crashed into Chesapeake Bay on a practice flight and was lost.

Below right:
Model of the Piaggio Pc7, showing the main and tail hydrofoils, the eliptical wing mounted high on the fuselage, the water propeller and rudder.
Rinaldo Piaggio SpA

this appellation not for its appearance, which was not exceptional, but more for its uncertain temperament, because, although it made a successful first flight, thereafter it became truculent. First its 1,000hp Fiat AS5 engine caught fire in the air, damaging the airframe; then it refused to get airborne. When it did, it leapt into the air and almost immediately stalled, dropping back on to the water, smashing off the floats and sinking.

The 'bad' Savoia Marchetti S65 flattered to deceive. A visually appealing design in which the pilot sat in a central nacelle between two 1,050hp Isotta Fraschini Asso engines in a push me-pull you arrangement, the S65 not only killed its test pilot, Warrant Officer Dal Molin, but, initially, engine cooling was insufficient to allow both engines to run together, an undesirable feature in a twin-engined aircraft! It was removed from the list.

The Piaggio-Pegna Pc7, which was 'impossible', was a craft which changed its mind and its role in operation; moreover, it required the man in the cockpit to be helmsman at one moment and pilot the next — and to have at least three hands and preferably four! Hydrofoils replaced the conventional floats, buoyancy being provided by the fuselage, or hull, which floated with the wings just clear of the water. Its 970hp Isotta Fraschini engine drove the airscrew through a long shaft and clutch mechanism housed in the very long nose. A similar clutch and shaft at the rear of the engine drove a marine screw. For take-off all power was applied to the marine screw to propel the Pc7 like a boat. When the nose rose out of the water on the hydrofoils, power was gradually transferred to the airscrew, which was braked in the horizontal position during the initial take-off stage, and the Pc7 became an aeroplane. At least that was the theory. One can imagine the pilot's problems: steering a straight course with the water rudder; holding the control column with the right hand; juggling the throttle with the left while; somehow, two more levers were pushed or pulled to declutch the marine screw and engage the airscrew. Little wonder that the Pc7 did not make the journey to Calshot for the 1929 contest.

And so to the ultimate Schneider. We know the winner, but what of the non-starters? France removed its name from the list when neither the Dewoitine HD412, the Bernard HV120 and 220 nor the Nieuport-Delage ND650 were ready in time to compete. Italy followed suit when its magnificent Macchi-Castoldi MC72 experienced temporarily insoluble problems with its big 2,850hp Fiat AS6 engine. This monster power unit was, in reality, two AS5s coupled in tandem on a common crankcase but each operating independently and powering one half of a counter-rotating propeller unit. Nevertheless, like the Gloster VI in 1929, the MC72 went on to set a new Absolute Speed Record of 440.681mph on 23 October 1934, a record for floatplanes which is still held by Italy. A lone German project was a Dornier flying boat with twin engines in the hull driving a four-blade pusher propeller mounted high on a pylon.

So what were the benefits of the vast investment of lives — 12 pilots were killed during test and practice, seven of them Italian — or time, money and effort in the 12 Schneider Contests. All countries gained something; it was the use to which they put these results which made the investment of value or not. In this respect perhaps Great Britain gained more than the other nations. The easiest dividend to quantify and qualify was the rapid development of reliable and efficient high-powered aero-engines. Those first Gnome rotary engines of 1913 produced one horsepower for every 1lb of engine weight and 5hp per 1,000cc capacity. By 1931 the weight per horsepower of the Rolls-Royce R engine used in the trophy-winning Supermarine S6B, was a little over nine ounces and it produced 75hp per 1,000cc and a total of 2,600hp. The development of special fuels for these engines was another benefit. Arthur Sidgreaves, Rolls-Royce Managing Director wrote in September 1931 in response to a critical letter: 'It is not too much to say that the research for the Schneider Trophy over the past two years is what our aero-engine department would otherwise have taken six to 10 years to learn'. By then it would have been too late, for there would have been no Battle of Britain to be won.

The second benefit was that the contests gave manufacturers a target and a reason to design and, more importantly, to build airframes intended for high speed flight. As a result Britain, France, Italy and the United States all learned much about metal construction, geared flight control systems, propeller design and engine testing.

Thirdly, these specialist seaplanes gave what was, necessarily, a small number of pilots the experience of flying high speed aircraft. It is doubtful, however, whether this was of great general benefit as their handling characteristics and control requirements were to prove very different from the later generations of fighter aircraft.

Without doubt the greatest and most traceable dividends from any country's Schneider Contest investment were the Spitfires and Hurricanes of

Below:
Incorrectly rigged aileron control cables precipitated the crash of the Short-Bristow Crusader during the flight trials for the 1927 contest in Venice. *Shorts*

Royal Air Force Fighter Command which played an early and vital role in the defence of the British Isles in the Battle of Britain during the summer of 1940. The design of their Rolls-Royce Merlin engines drew heavily on that of the R engine, and the Merlin's success stemmed directly from Rolls-Royce's experience with the racing engine. Similarly, the knowledge which R. J. Mitchell gained in his design of the Supermarine floatplanes for the last four contests was of inestimable value when he designed first the Supermarine Type 224, then the Type 300 which became the Spitfire. One final long-term beneficial result from Britain's investment was the centrifugal compressor of Frank Whittle's turbojet engine of 1938 which was reputed to have been based on the unit used in the Rolls-Royce R racing engine.

Some 30 years after the Battle of Britain, Sir George Edwards, then Chairman and Managing Director of the British Aircraft Corporation, wrote 'If the industry had been limited during those inter-war years to design studies alone and had not been able to translate ideas into hardware by actually building aeroplanes, it is certain that such successful fighters as the Spitfire and Hurricane would not have emerged'.

Above:
The Gloster VI heads for the water at Calshot in early September 1929, before engine problems prevented it going to the start line at Calshot.

Below:
One of the pair of Macchi M67s which retired in the second lap of the 1929 contest.

Alan J. Wright

Family Planning

Over 20 years have passed since a group of major European operators began to formulate a specification for a new generation airliner. Although no firm conclusions were reached, at least it was agreed that its capacity should cater for about 225 passengers. For many months the whole project was in jeopardy while awaiting the outcome of international political bickering, much of the procrastination originating from the British government. Insistence on the use of the Rolls-Royce RB207 or RB211 engines was one of the main stumbling blocks, the power plants not really favoured by the French who were in overall control. At last there was a glimmer of hope in 1970. A General Election was held in Britain which was expected to produce more enthusiastic support. But it was not to be. The new government was no longer the sympathetic, Opposition. Instead it was determined to cut public spending drastically, with the result that with great firmness the axe was wielded to detach itself from any further involvement in the joint venture. In many ways it saved the aircraft, since with the way now clear, Airbus Industrie was formed in December 1970. The new company consisted of Aérospatiale, Deutsche Airbus and Fokker-VFW. Ironically Britain still contributed some 20% of the production work as Hawker Siddeley had already been contracted to design and build the wing at Chester.

Fortunately throughout the arguments, plans for the A300 had continued steadily, faithfully supported by Air France's design contributions and comments. During the period the machine had grown in size quite significantly, a feature which did not please everyone. It was therefore inevitable, with the uncertainty surrounding the type, that the initial sales success rate was poor. Against this unfavourable background, the first A300 was duly produced and after successful trials flew its inaugural scheduled service between Paris and Heathrow on 23 May 1974. As the German national carrier, Lufthansa was expected to set a good example by selecting the type for its fleet. After a considerable delay, a token order was given, but the airline expressed a far greater interest in something capable of carrying about 200 seats rather than the 253 of the A300. It considered this number to be unnecessary for its type of operation. Hence it was February 1976 before the first of its aircraft was delivered.

Despite the obvious potential, Airbus Industrie remained non-committal about the scaled-down model, since it was only one of several options under review. One of the easiest and cheapest methods to arrive at the desired size was to remove 7m from the fuselage, leaving that remainder of the structure largely unchanged. Such a scheme was not acceptable to Lufthansa, in all probability the launch customer. In that airline's opinion a new wing was essential if operating costs were to benefit from the latest technical advances. Jointly, Swissair and Lufthansa began to compile a specification which by, March 1978, was encouraging Airbus to devote more attention to the type. A year later orders from the two

airlines provided the incentive for work to begin on the detailed design and construction of the A300B10, which now became officially redesignated as the A310. By this time Britain was directly involved in the affairs of Airbus since a 20% share had been taken in the consortium.

Following its first flight in April 1982, the new type's flight development was uneventfully completed, allowing deliveries to begin in March 1983. Lufthansa's first revenue-earning flight with its A310s was made on 10 April and as more were received, so the larger A300s were withdrawn thereby fulfilling the German airline's long-expressed wish. Fellow launch customer, Swissair, was not far behind, introducing its first machine into service on 21 April. At the same time the carrier announced that it had modified its original order for 10 A310s so that four of them would be the proposed 300 Series extended-range version.

Below left:
Trans European's OO-TEF, an A300-B1, was used as the second test airframe before entering service.
George W. Pennick

Above:
The shorter fuselage of this Pan Am A310 can readily be seen in this plan view. *Peter R. March*

Below:
An early operator of the A300-B4 was Alitalia.
Peter R. March

This latest addition to the expanding Family confirmed Airbus Industrie's policy of keeping up with the demands of the airlines by offering a competitor for the comparable Boeing 767ER. To achieve the required performance, several technologically advanced features were built into the design. Space for an extra five tonnes of fuel was found in the tailplane, but not purely as a store. By using it as a trim tank, drag could be reduced while cruising, by minimising the lift required from the wing. This principle of adjusting the centre of gravity position in flight by the transfer of fuel was used on Concorde, but the A310-300 became the first production sub-sonic airliner to employ the system. Considerable success was gained in weight saving by using carbon fibre reinforced plastic for the construction of the fin, again a pioneering step. Carbon brakes brought a reduction of 1,000lb (500kg), improved aluminium alloys in the wings contributed 330lb (150kg), while more surprisingly the substitution of metric standard electric cables for the original Imperial type brought some 640lb (175kg) of savings. It seems rather strange that Airbus should have ever accepted anything other than France's normal unit of measure in the first place. It all helped to give a similar empty weight to that of the earlier A310, while at the same time increasing the maximum take-off weight by some eight tonnes. With 218 passengers in a typical first and economy class layout, a range of 4,600 miles (8,500km) became possible, which was about 800 miles (1,500km) farther than the Series 200 could manage.

Flight trials of the first aircraft began on 8 July 1985 when F-WWCA was taken on its maiden trip by chief test pilot Pierre Baud. Such

was its behaviour that during the 5½hr sortie, a maximum speed of Mach 0.84 was reached at 41,000ft. Fuel transfer tests were also initiated, the first really practical trials of the new feature that had been possible. By the end of the month almost 50hr of the 220hr of flying time allocated for the test programme had been completed. With everything proceeding satisfactorily, certification of the Pratt & Whitney JT9D-7R4 powered version was expected in December. The test airframe remained with the manufacturer, but Swissair received its first Series 300 registered HB-IPF shortly after, quickly followed by three others. Middle East and West African services were scheduled to be handled by these aircraft, replacing DC-10-30s on the routes.

Early in 1986 the Series 300 powered by General Electric CF6-80C2 engines gained its certificate. Since most of the airframe's flying characteristics had been explored by the first prototype, most of the work involved for the second machine was concerned with the engines. Accordingly only 160hr or so was needed to complete the trials. Air India was the first customer to receive this variant, deliveries starting in April. In this case the airline's ageing Boeing 707s were replaced, the A310s taking over some of the European sectors which were unable to support the much larger capacity Boeing 747s.

From the spring of 1986, all A310s produced included the improvements built in to the Series 300, since not all carriers were in need of a long range capability, but were only too pleased to save on costs with enhanced performance. With the weight savings derived from such items as the plastic fin and carbon brakes, the Series 200 became 7% more fuel efficient than the first aircraft off the line in 1983. Nevertheless this variant has proved extremely flexible in operation, taking short sectors such as Lufthansa's Frankfurt-Stuttgart (90 miles/160km) and Amsterdam-Heathrow (200 miles/370km) with KLM, in its stride. On the other hand, routes up to 3,000 miles are also flown by the aircraft belonging to other operators.

When the A310 was originally introduced, many of its new features were applied to the A300. This resulted in the Series 600, basically a model 300 but with the redesigned rear

Below:
The long-range A310-300 made its first flight on 8 July 1985 powered by two Pratt & Whitney JT9D-7R4 engines. *Airbus Industrie*

Right:
Air India was the first customer for the CF6-80C2 powered version of the A310-300, which made its first flight on 6 September 1985. *Airbus Industrie*

Below right:
Flying since March 1984, the A300-600 testbed has since been used for the certification programme with CF6-80C2 engines. *Airbus Industrie*

INDIA

A300-600
A300
Airbus Industrie
F-WZLR

KUWAIT

Above left:
Kuwait Airways became the launch customer for the convertible version of the A300-600. *Airbus Industrie*

Left:
Assembly of A300s takes place on a common line at Toulouse, after the various sections are flown in from factories all over Europe. *Airbus Industrie*

Above:
The four Super Guppies have an essential role in A300/A310 production. Eight flights are necessary to ferry all sections of one complete airliner to Toulouse.
Peter R. March

fuselage of the A310. It was then possible to include two extra rows of seats thereby increasing the capacity in a standard mixed class to 267. More containers could also be stowed in the hold. Overall refinements of this design whittled away over two tonnes from the aircraft's weight, while the flight deck was updated with cathode ray tube (CRT) displays for a two man crew option.

Sales of this type were fairly slow at first, principally due to the demand for such large machines falling during the slack years of the early 1980s, plus a stock of unsold A300B4s. Saudia and Kuwait Airways began using their Pratt & Whitney powered aircraft in 1984, Thai Airways International becoming the first operator to receive the General Electric version in September 1985. With an order from Lufthansa during the year for seven 600s for early 1987 delivery plus options on a further three, there were signs that the type's fortunes were becoming more encouraging.

It was a good moment to offer a longer range version of this model to be known as the A300-600R. When announcing the variant in late 1985, Airbus expected the aircraft to be ready for service entry at the end of 1987, provided that a sufficient number of customers was obtained to enable the programme to be launched during 1986. Weight reduction and the extra range would be achieved in a similar manner to that of the A310, likewise the engine choice would rest with the CF6-80C2 and the new Pratt & Whitney PW4000, both types giving greater thrust to maintain performance.

So far all of Airbus Industrie's products had been wide-bodied airliners to the same general pattern, but it did not mean that the company had forgotten that a market existed for other sizes. On the contrary, from the mid-1970s long-term studies had been in progress to investigate new ranges, one of which was known as the single aisle (SA) series. It was intended that two versions of a narrow-bodied airliner would be offered using the type designations of SA1 and SA2. Dimensionally similar, they would vary in capacity and range.

By 1981 the proposed aircraft had been renumbered as the A320-100 and -200 respectively, a move which was interpreted as a definite indication that Airbus was about to launch its new creation as the next member of the family. Development costs of this brand-new design were expected almost to equal the joint expense of the two wide-bodied derivatives known as the TA9 and TA11 (twin aisle), currently receiving equal priority from the planners. Regardless of which was chosen to be the next product from the Toulouse line, there was plenty of scope for another partner to join the group, especially if the necessary financial backing could not be raised by the existing members.

Details of the A320 were revealed at the 1981 Paris Salon, confirming that it would be capable of carrying about 160 passengers in a single aisle cabin. At the same time the manufacturer was able to announce a preliminary contract

A320

1st
A320
WING
FROM BRITISH AEROSPACE CHESTER
3 WEEKS AHEAD OF SCHEDULE

with Air France for 50 aircraft, 25 of which were options. This act of faith by the French carrier no doubt raised Airbus Industrie's spirits, but still it was not in a position actually to launch the type, mainly due to the continuing lack of financial support from within the consortium. By the time of the next Salon in 1983, the A320 differed considerably from the early design. Basically it remained the same shape, but the airframe had shed 2.4 tonnes and the fuselage had shrunk in length by 1.3m. Further reduction in wing area had helped in the quest for weight savings, while the powerplant had become a pair of CFM56-4s giving 23,000lb thrust. Composite materials were extensively used, with both the fin and tailplane abandoning the conventional aluminium alloy in order to become 20% lighter.

At last, in October 1983, another definite order was received, this time from British Caledonian. This operator's example was followed in December by the Yugoslavian airline Inex Adria, the pair bringing the prospect of a launch date much nearer. Money was, alas, still a missing commodity, since neither of the other major partners, Germany and the UK, had committed themselves. Fortunately a ray of

Top left:
The forthcoming narrow-body A320 seen in model form.
Airbus Industrie

Far left:
British Aerospace removed the first A320 wingbox from the jigs at Chester on 3 October 1985, three weeks ahead of schedule. *British Aerospace*

Left:
At the same time the cockpit and nose was taking shape at Aérospatiale's St Nazaire factory. *Airbus Industrie*

Above:
The new technology cockpit of the A320 replaces traditional instruments by electronic monitoring displayed on cathode ray tubes; the control column is replaced by a small side-mounted joystick.
Airbus Industrie

Above:
The side-stick was first installed in the A300 test airframe, and gave no serious problems. *Airbus Industrie*

hope was generated in Germany when the government transferred DM12 million (£3 million) to Airbus as a token gesture towards the end of 1983. This was backed up in March by an interest-free loan of £390 million, leaving only Britain to add its contribution. Eventually and only just in time, British Aerospace was granted a £250 million deferred-interest loan which although only 57% of the requested sum, left the company not too unhappy at the arrangement despite having to find another £200 million from its own resources. Formally the A320 was launched in March 1984.

Apart from the details already released, it was now revealed that the cabin width would be 19cm (7.6in) greater than other airliners seating six-abreast. This modest growth would permit greater flexibility with the layout, giving operators the option of wider seats, wider aisle or a combination of both in a five-abreast configuration. Another important benefit from the airlines' viewpoint was that the underfloor containers would have the same base size as the standard LD3 type.

When introduced on to the flight deck of the A310, CRT display replacement of the normal electro-mechanical instruments was a major step forward, which in turn paved the way for two-man crew operation. Naturally the A320 inherited this philosophy, but in addition Airbus proposed this time to remove the time honoured pilot's control column in favour of a small stick mounted on the side of the cockpit. This revolutionary system was duly installed in the A300 test airframe F-WUAD, although in this case only the left-hand seat was so equipped. No problems were experienced during the 75hr of trials, with all those involved finding the 12in-long stick easy to handle and very precise. This confirmation left the way clear for the A320 to be similarly controlled.

Using fly-by-wire techniques, for much of the time the aircraft will be under the command of the electronic flight control system (EFCS). Its computers are programmed so that they will not allow overspeeding, stalling or other violent manoeuvres. Commands are made by means of electrical pulses to signal requirements to the control surfaces, therefore virtually eliminating the need for cables and pulleys. Back-up mechanical power is provided for the rudder and tailplane trim, which in the unlikely event of total electronic failure, will give adequate control while the fault is rectified. Such a loss could result from lightning strikes since sudden electrical surges are not appreciated by computers however sophisticated. Airbus has built in protection against this possibility by encasing all wiring looms with a metal shielding in unpressurised areas. Local earthing points have been avoided and all wires have been twisted to prevent differential voltages being set up. Since there is no mechanical link between the two side-sticks, an interesting situation can be envisaged if the pilots have opposing views on direction. In these circumstances the EFCS cancels the instructions before the aircraft is split down the middle, to await something more sensible. Should both sticks request the same move, then in this case the effect is doubled. These conditions only apply when normal control changes are sought. Anything outside the acceptable limits will be ignored by the EFCS. It means that the more intelligent pilot wins, not the stronger. Both are advised of the changing events by means of a series of captions displayed in front of them, so there should be no doubt as to which is in control.

By mid-1985, construction of the first A320 was well under way, as usual spread around the various factories of the consortium. The wing centre section began its journey to Toulouse by travelling to MBB's Hamburg site on 1 July from its birth place at Nantes. The German company had already started production of the components for the rear fuselage, which, when completed, was joined to the centre section

Below:
Airbus Industrie's first four-engined project is the TA11, shown in this model. *Airbus Industrie*

before being flown to Toulouse as a single unit in March 1986. Meanwhile at Chester, British Aerospace had been building the first pair of A320 wing boxes, which in December were transported to Bristol/Filton. Here, all system, slats, flaps and ailerons were added before being flown by Super Guppy to join the rest of the aircraft at the main Airbus plant. To accommodate the future flow, construction of a new production centre was begun during 1985, with a planned operational date of October 1986.

Everything was on course for the scheduled first flight in the spring of 1987, as well as preparing for series production of the type. It will be the CFM56-5 version which will carry out the initial trials, the engine chosen by the launch customers. Airbus later offered the International Aero Engines (IAE) V2500 as an alternative, this variant due to become airborne in the autumn of 1988 in readiness for airline service in the following spring. Both are new engines and were programmed for their inaugural runs in the early part of 1986. At that time over 100 firm orders had been received for the A320 from a growing number of customers, including Air France, Air Inter, Ansett Airlines, British Caledonian, Cyprus Airways, Indian Airlines, Inex Adria, Lufthansa and Pan American.

Surprisingly the Airbus 150-seater will not have a direct Boeing competitor for some years since the American company does not consider there will be sufficient advances in technology before 1992 to make it worthwhile. By that year, however, Boeing expects to introduce a propfan powered airliner in the same class, but much development is still needed to produce the proof of the economies claimed for this type of engine. By then the A320 should be well established.

Of the other projects actively under consideration at Toulouse, the TA11 is the first to break away from the Airbus preference for twins. With its four engines, it is intended as a long range derivative of the A300 Series offering between 240 and 280 seats. A range of 5,400 miles is expected which would give it comparable seat/mile costs with the present Boeing 747 despite being only half the size. Whether the go-ahead is given depends on the receipt of 50-60 orders for a start, but in this class the Airbus machine will be lined up alongside the MD-11, Boeing 767ER and the 747-400. Whatever happens to the TA11, the company now has a family to meet airlines' needs, commonality between the types being the key.

Below:
The development A300 Airbus landing at Farnborough.
Peter R. March

Above:
Iberia's A300B4 Airbus EC-DNR *Ordesa* touches down at Bristol-Lulsgate. *Peter R. March*

Below:
British Caledonian Airways operates Airbus A310-203 G-BKWU. *Peter R. March*

Harrier Profile

The vectored thrust Harrier, still the free world's only operational V/STOL (Vertical/Short Take-Off and Landing) aircraft, has revolutionised the deployment of tactical air power from land and sea. In service with the Royal Air Force, United States Marine Corps and Spanish Navy, the Harrier is powered by a Pegasus engine of 21,500lb (96.6kN) thrust and is capable of operating from virtually any land site or from the decks of small ships, in almost any conditions.

The prototype V/STOL aircraft, the Hawker P1127, made its first flight (a hover) on 21 October 1960 and was followed by the Kestrel which flew on 7 March 1964. The first production model of the Harrier was airborne on 31 August 1966.

Today the RAF has three operational Harrier squadrons, two at Gutersloh in West Germany (Nos 3 and 4) and one at RAF Wittering (No 1), together with the Operational Conversion Unit (No 233 OCU). Similarly the US Marine Corps has three front line Harrier (designated AV-8A in US service) units together with a training squadron. The Spanish Navy also operates the aircraft, renaming it the Matador (designated

Below:
Four development Hawker P1127s were built at Kingston. The fourth (XP984) shown here was built to Kestrel standard, with a Pegasus 5 engine. *Rolls-Royce*

Bottom:
The first of nine Kestrel FGA1s (XS688) which was operated by the Tripartite Trials Squadron at West Raynham from 15 October 1964 to 30 November 1965. *Bristol Siddeley*

Top:
The first production batch of Harrier GR1s left the Kingston production line from December 1967. The fifth aircraft XV742 shown here, was used as a demonstrator registered G-VSTO. *Rolls-Royce*

Above:
XV279 was the fourth of six pre-production Harrier GR1s, making its first flight from Kingston on 4 March 1967.
Rolls-Royce

AV-8S) and operating one squadron from its base at Rota or from its carriers *Dedalo* and *Principe de Asturias*.

The Harrier was designed to operate with maximum effectiveness from small unprepared fields and forward sites on land and from ships at sea, in the fighter, ground attack, and reconnaissance roles. It was to fulfil these last two requirements that a total of 14 RAF Harrier GR3s were deployed to the Falklands in 1982 operating from the RN Carrier HMS *Hermes*. Most of the RAF pilots had never launched from a carrier deck and 'Ski-jump' prior to this.

To perform its duties, the Harrier has been cleared to use a very wide range of British, American and standard NATO ordnance. Rockets, cluster bombs, free-fall and retarded bombs as well as 30mm guns are the principal weapons for ground attack. All Harrier variants can carry Sidewinder infra-red homing missiles

Above:
A flight of US Marine Corps AV-8A Harriers. *Rolls-Royce*

Below:
A development AV-8 getting airborne on a test flight in the USA.

Top left:
Harrier GR1s went into RAF service in 1969 with No 1 Squadron at RAF Wittering. *Rolls-Royce*

Above left:
By 1972 three squadrons (Nos 3, 4 and 20) were operating the V/STOL ground attack fighter in Germany. Here a GR1 from No 20 Squadron is operating from a 'hide' near Wildenrath. *Rolls-Royce*

Left:
A bomb- and cannon-equipped GR1 of No 4 Squadron over picturesque West German scenery. *Rolls-Royce*

Above:
The RAF's Harriers were up-dated, with new electronics, laser rangefinder in the nose and more powerful Pegasus engines, to become the Harrier GR3, with a new distinctive profile. *Rolls-Royce*

for the air-defence role. RAF Harriers are fitted with the Ferranti FE541 Inertial Navigation and Attack Systems (INAS) and the Smiths Industries Head-Up Display (HUD). The HUD forms a complete flight information panel in itself and, in the head-down navigation display, the principal feature is an optically-projected moving map. RAF Harriers are also fitted with Laser Ranging and Marked Target Seeker equipment. This pinpoints and measures range to the target by infra-red light, for more accurate and rapid weapon delivery. They also carry a Radar Warning Receiver and UHF/VHF radios — as well as navaids such as TACAN, UHF Homer and IFF. The two-seat Harrier can be used for operational V/STOL training and as a combat aircraft flown solo or with both seats occupied. It is fitted with the same operational equipment as the single-seat and can carry identical weapons through the same missions.

622

04

Left:
A ground crewman checks readiness of an AGM-65E Laser Maverick on a Marine Corps AV-8B Harrier II.

Below left:
A RAF Harrier GR3 of No 1 Squadron based at Wittering, Northants. *Peter R. March*

Below:
The US Marine Corps AV-8Bs operate from vessels at sea as well as shore bases. *Rolls-Royce*

The Sea Harrier FRS1 was designed to meet a Royal Navy requirement for a V/STOL fighter/reconnaissance/strike aircraft to operate at sea from the RN's new carriers, HMS *Invincible*, *Illustrious*, and *Ark Royal*. Built by the Weybridge Division of British Aerospace, the Sea Harrier first flew on 20 August 1978 from Dunsfold. The Sea Harrier proved itself in combat in 1982, when a total of 28 were deployed to the South Atlantic during Operation 'Corporate'. Operating from HMS *Hermes* and *Invincible*, the Sea Harriers provided air cover for the Task Force and the land forces ashore.

Above:
The Harrier first went to sea in the early 70s when pre-production aircraft XV281 was operated from HMS *Eagle*. *Fleet Air Arm Museum*

Below:
A Harrier GR3 of No 3 Squadron lifts off from a concealed forest site.

Derived from the Royal Air Force's Harrier GR3, Sea Harrier's avionics differ by about 90% in comparison, and feature equipment changes to suit its roles and missions, as well as the more hostile environment imposed by operations at sea. Its airframe, powerplant and mechanical systems are broadly similar. The Sea Harrier's primary equipment differences from the earlier RAF variant include a larger

Head-Up Display driven by a 20,000 word digital computer, which not only generates display symbology but also functions as a very flexible air-to-air and air-to-surface weapon aiming computer. It has a self-aligning attitude and heading reference platform, controlled by a digital computer which performs all the navigation and endurance functions. The platform is cross-referenced to a Doppler radar.

Currently, the primary external sensor, the Ferranti Blue Fox radar, is derived from the Seaspray radar used in the RN Lynx helicopter, extensively modified to provide the air-to-air and air-to-surface modes demanded by the Sea Harrier's operational tasks. The radar display is a TV-raster daylight-viewing tube which conveys flight information as well as the radar data to the pilot. It also has a radar altimeter and improved radar warning system, as well as a simple autopilot to reduce pilot workload by providing attitude, heading and height-hold facilities. Provision is also made to carry

Above:
When operating in Norway on winter exercises the Harrier GR3s of No 1 Squadron are given a temporary camouflage befitting the background.

Below:
The US Marine Corps also received eight two-seat trainers. *Rolls-Royce*

Above:
An unusual view of a US Marine Corps AV-8A making a vertical take-off from a carrier. *Rolls-Royce*

Below:
The huge air intakes for the Rolls-Royce Pegasus engine are shown clearly as a RAF Harrier GR3 takes off.
Rolls-Royce

air-to-surface stand-off missiles. The Royal Navy is introducing the BAe Sea Eagle anti-shipping missile, although other ASMs, such as Harpoon, can be carried.

BAe is currently undertaking a Sea Harrier mid-life update programme to take advantage of new missiles and avionic systems. The modifications include a new Ferranti pulse Doppler radar for a 'look-down/shoot-down' capability, in conjunction with AMRAAM, an improved radar warning receiver and a revised cockpit display with full digital data-bus.

The first Sea Harrier FRS1 was delivered to the RN in June 1979. A total of 48 Sea Harriers plus four T4N two-seat trainers was subsequently ordered for service with three squadrons: No 899 Headquarters and Training Squadron and Nos 800 and 801 Naval Air squadrons at RNAS Yeovilton.

The Indian Navy has received six Sea Harrier FRS51s and two two-seat T60 trainers for No 300 (White Tiger) Naval Air Squadron. This unit became fully operational early in 1985. A further order for 10 single-seat FRS51s and one two-seat T60 was placed in November 1985.

Harrier II is the most advanced version of the Harrier produced to date. Developed jointly by British Aerospace and McDonnell Douglas in the USA, the Harrier II is in service with the United States Marine Corps. The first USMC Harrier II (designated AV-8B) was handed over to US Marine Corps Air Station, Cherry Point, North Carolina in December 1983.

Assembly of the Harrier II in the UK takes place primarily at British Aerospace's Kingston, Brough, Hamble and Dunsfold factories. A total of 238 Harrier IIs are programmed for the US Marine Corps and 62 Harrier IIs, (GR Mk 5) are required by the Royal Air Force.

The Harrier II differs considerably from its predecessors in that it has a new supercritical aerofoil wing with a greater area and span which contains more than 2,000lb additional internal fuel. The main wing torque box structure is manufactured of carbon fibre composite with metal leading edges. It also has large CFC slotted flaps and ailerons whose movement is linked with nozzle deflection at STO (Short Take-Off) unstick, to provide greater wing lift capability enabling operation at the much higher all-up weight. Further, longitudinal strakes and a lateral fence (LIDS — Lift Improvement Devices) have been incorporated on the under-fuselage gun pod system to capture ground-reflected jets in VTOL (Vertical Take-Off and Landing) to give a bigger ground cushion and reduce hot gas re-circulation. The Harrier II also has Leading

Top:
Sea Harriers, ordered in 1975, were first delivered to the Fleet Air Arm at Yeovilton in 1979.

Above:
The Spanish Navy placed an initial order for six single-seat AV-8S Matadors in 1975. Together with a further five aircraft they have been operated from Rota and the carrier *Dedalo*. *Rolls-Royce*

Top right:
Three squadrons are equipped with Sea Harrier FRS1s: No 800 NAS (nearest camera), No 801 NAS (centre) and No 899 NAS (behind). No 809 NAS also operated the fighter during the Falklands conflict. *Rolls-Royce*

Above right:
The Harrier T4N is used for pilot training by No 899 NAS at Yeovilton. *Peter R. March*

Right:
An Indian Navy Sea Harrier getting airborne in 1984. A follow-on order was placed towards the end of 1985.
Peter R. March

ROYAL NAVY
000
ROYAL NAVY
127

ROYAL NAVY

NAVY

Above:
Significant improvements have been made to the RAF's Harrier GR5 shown here on an early flight. *BAe Kingston*

Below:
A Royal Navy Sea Harrier FRS1 getting airborne from the 'ski-jump' at Yeovilton. *Rolls-Royce*

Below:
The new GR5 has nearly double the payload/radius of the RAF's Harrier GR3s. *BAe Kingston*

Above:
The first Harrier II (AV-8B) making its first ski-ramp take-off. *Rolls-Royce*

Below:
A US Marine Corps AV-8B taking off from USN Patuxent River, on a test mission with an AGM-65E Laser Maverick under the wing. *McDonnell Douglas*

Edge Root Extensions (LERX) to enhance its air combat agility by improving turn rate and a raised cockpit with a bubble canopy to improve pilot view and to provide additional space for avionics.

RAF GR5s differ from the USMC's AV-8Bs in that they are to be equipped to meet the demands for the Harrier's close support role in central Europe. To facilitate their low altitude high speed missions in European weather, a moving map display is incorporated in the cockpit and there are also avionic equipment changes to meet the RAF's operational requirements. The UK aircraft also have two additional underwing weapon stations (making a total of nine) ahead of the outrigger wheels. These additional stores are solely for the carriage of Sidewinder air-to-air missiles for self-defence/interception. Other equipment selected for the GR5 includes a Martin Baker ejection seat, a radar warning receiver, an infra-red reconnaissance sensor and systems monitoring to provide for post-sortie de-briefing and preventive maintenance.

Powered by the Rolls-Royce Pegasus 105, the GR5 will be able to fly nearly double the payload/radius of the current RAF GR3. Its maximum external payload will be over 9,000lb and will include a full range of standard UK, US and NATO ordnance, as does the GR3.

Brymon – UK's first STOL-line

March 1987 is the 18th anniversary of the formation of Brymon Aviation by New Zealander Bill Bryce and Chris Amon one time leader of the Ferrari motor-racing team. Eighteen years in which the original company first based at Thruxton, progressed from being a Cessna sales outlet, moved to Fairoaks to run the local School of Flying, took on ad-hoc charter flying, moved to Newquay and then Plymouth as a scheduled airline, became the first UK operator of the DHC Twin Otter and Dash 7, took over the operation and later purchased its base at Plymouth Airport and is now poised to become the UK's first real STOL operator when it starts flying into the new London Dockland STOL in mid-1987, Brymon Airways, as it was retitled, today operates the most southerly fixed-wing route in the UK to the Scilly Isles and the most northerly route from Aberdeen to Unst. Between these two routes it also flies the longest non-stop scheduled air route in Britain, with the once-a-week Plymouth-Aberdeen service. It also remains unique in being the only regional airline in the UK to have an entire fleet of STOL aircraft (Dash 7s and Twin Otters). All this has not been achieved without considerable problems, the most serious of which was financial insolvency which hit the airline in 1983 and put it within a stroke of extinction.

Above:
A Dash 7 at Unst, the UK's most northerly airliner terminal. *Brymon Airways*

Below:
Brymon's two STOL-liner types, Twin Otter and Dash 7, in front of the Plymouth Airport terminal. *Andrew March*

Bottom:
Viewed from the flight deck of Twin Otter G-BIHO, the tiny airstrip at St Mary's, Isles of Scilly, the most southerly UK airport. *Peter R. March*

Above:
Brymon's brightly painted DHC Dash 7 G-BRYB landing at Heathrow. *Peter R. March*

Above right:
Twin Otters like G-BWRB are used for services to the Isles of Scilly and on low density routes. *Peter R. March*

1983 was a traumatic year for Brymon Airways, seeing the resignation of its Chairman and Chief Executive, Bill Bryce and the ownership passing to a consortium including De Havilland Canada with a majority 80% holding.

The airline's Chairman and Chief Executive, ex-British Airways Board member Charles Stuart, who has steered the rescue, explains how the company came back from the brink of disaster. Mr Stuart first outlines the scale of the problem that faced him when he took up his appointment on 17 October 1983. 'In the early part of 1983 the company faced losses of about £3 million, largely as a result of sterling's weakness which considerably altered the interest charges on the purchase of our three Dash 7s, and some inept financial management, rather than trading losses. In the financial year ending 31 March 1983 we carried 130,000 passengers, a growth of more than 20% over 1982. Nevertheless, it was a precarious situation which demanded prompt action. A management committee ran the company from April through to October and in the six months to 30 September it was ahead of financial targets, making an operating profit and well on the way to meeting borrowing costs.

'I came in as Chairman and Chief Executive with the task of reconstructing the company through the transitional period with the objective of achieving improved business, providing stronger management, financial restructuring and closer cost control. It was an unusual situation. I was a minority shareholder (only 5%) but I had full responsibility. This was because the principal shareholder, DHC, is based in Canada and under UK regulations a foreign company is not permitted to control a UK airline. Under a special agreement with the CAA and DHC, I had until the end of 1985 to get things properly sorted out, as by that time DHC wanted UK or EEC funding for the majority shareholding. The subsequent investment by British Airways and the management purchase of the remaining DHC equity leaves us in a strong position for expansion in 1987 to meet the challenge of being the prime operators from the London City Stolport'.

Bill Bryce, joint founder of the company, who resigned as Chairman and Chief Executive on 17 October 1983, subsequently withdrew all his interest in Brymon Airways in December that year. His shareholding passed to the new consortium and he returned to his native New Zealand where he set up a company to provide consultancy services for Stolports worldwide.

The 15 years that he built up and controlled Brymon Aviation Airways are a dramatic example of what hard work and enthusiasm can achieve; and at the same time underline how it can be brought to the edge of failure by factors outside any individual's control. He started his aviation activities in the UK in March 1969 at Thruxton flying a Cessna 150 and 172 and soon afterwards became a Cessna dealer. He moved the company to Fairoaks in November 1969 after purchasing the Fairoaks School of Flying and 10 months later commenced ad hoc charter flying with Islander G-AXXJ which was delivered in September 1970.

With a change of name to Brymon Airways, Bryce obtained his first route licence to operate the Islander between Newquay and the Isles of Scilly, making the first flight on 15 June 1972. From that inauspicious beginning at the tiny civil terminal at RAF St Mawgan, Brymon Airways grew into a scheduled operation. For the first year, the company was based at Newquay, but as the route network grew, Plymouth became the new base. Route extensions were made linking Newquay and Plymouth with Jersey as well as the Scillies. In 1973 a second Islander (G-BADK) was added and the Exeter-Isles of Scilly route was inaugurated for the summer and Plymouth-Morlaix (Brittany) linked from 2 November. Earlier in the year Guernsey had also been added to the network. The next major development came in April 1974 when Brymon became the first UK purchaser of the DHC Twin Otter with the delivery of factory fresh G-BDHC painted in the airline's striking yellow and blue colour scheme. To cope with the still expanding services a third Islander (G-AZEI) was leased between April and December from Doug Arnold. A novel step was taken in June 1975 when a new route from Plymouth to Cork was opened up using Cessna 337 G-BACF. In the same year Islander G-BAVT was leased from Intra Airways to augment the fleet.

With the introduction of the twice daily Newquay-Heathrow service using the ex-British Midland Airways Herald G-ATIG in 1977 and two years later the Plymouth-Gatwick route flying Twin Otters, Brymon could be said to have really arrived as a serious British airline, offering domestic and international scheduled routes. With the phasing out of the Islanders, a succession of Twin Otters has been operated, including G-BFGP from 1977, G-BGMC and G-BGMD from 1979, G-BGZP and G-BWRB from 1980 and G-BIHO from 1981. A further aircraft, LN-WFC was leased from Wideroes for the summer of 1983. The first Twin Otter G-BDHC was sold in 1980 for use by the Transglobe Expedition. The fleet diminished to just two of the type, G-BWRB and G-BIHO, in 1984.

The arrival of the first Dash 7, G-BRYC in July 1981 underlined the outstanding

Above:
Twin Otter G-BIHO awaiting passengers at St Mary's after a scheduled flight from Bristol. *Peter R. March*

Right:
Islander G-AXXJ was the first of the type to be flown by Brymon Airways from 1970. *Peter R. March*

Below right:
Herald G-ATIG was introduced in 1977 for the Newquay-Heathrow service. *Peter R. March*

achievement of Bill Bryce in winning the long-term charter operation of two Dash 7s for Chevron Oil linking Aberdeen and Unst. This was won in spite of fierce opposition from the established Scottish based airlines. A third Dash 7 was added in 1982 for schedules out of Plymouth and later that year replaced the Herald on the important Heathrow service from Newquay. This aircraft is well utilised operating on a daily schedule with up to five round trips between Plymouth/Newquay and Heathrow.

The Scottish operation, which commenced in September 1981, works like clockwork. Three scheduled round trips Monday-Saturday carry over 900 passengers a week for Chevron Petroleum between Aberdeen and Baltasound Airport, Unst. The Dash 7 is the only 50-seat aircraft that can operate into this, the UK's most northerly airport, with its 600m runway and minimum aids. The punctuality has been outstanding with 96% of all departures within 15min of schedule and a 99% technical despatch rate — which compares favourably with BA's Shuttle. The great advantage is having a modern, comfortable 50-seat aircraft which is well equipped and compares very well with a helicopter, particularly on the long over-water stretches. With Chevron Brymon built up a good working relationship, which was underlined when the airline was awarded a new 'open-ended' contract in 1985. 'We offer a very good service in rigorous conditions on competitive terms' is the way in which Charles Stuart describes the reason for the airline's success in the face of fierce competition from the other Scottish operators. The Saturday direct scheduled service between Aberdeen, Newquay and Plymouth, which was started in April 1983, is the longest non-stop scheduled air route in Britain and enables Brymon to rotate the Dash 7s for maintenance. The aircraft which comes to Plymouth stays for a week to operate the southern day-time schedules and enters the engineering hangar each night for the continuous maintenance programme. It returns to Aberdeen the following weekend.

Brymon's chairman has no doubts about the direction in which the airline will be heading: 'The London Stolport is a most imaginative aviation concept, which is thoroughly practical and might well be a forerunner of similar services elsewhere. I first examined the idea for

Top:
The first Dash 7 G-BRYC was delivered in July 1981, replacing the Herald on Heathrow services via Plymouth and for the important Chevron oil contract.
Peter R. March

Centre:
STOL Dash 7s are the only medium-sized airliners that can operate from Plymouth's short runway, and will be able to fly the new London STOL-port. *Peter R. March*

Above:
The STOL performance was shown by trial flights into London Dockland before the planning enquiry in 1984.
Brymon Airways

a regional Stolport (at Sheffield) back in 1969 when I was heading British Air Services. The lack of suitably sized aircraft, with only the Twin Otter and Short Skyliner then available, prevented a development from getting off the ground. Today the concept is eminently practicable with the 50-seat Dash 7 a well proven economic proposition. The picture for 1987 onwards looks very exciting with Brymon Airways now in a position that it can respond to these challenges and capitalise on the opportunities presented'.

There can be little doubt that Brymon Airways has the right experience, the right equipment as well as a keen and enthusiastic team to take full advantage of the opportunities that are likely to present themselves in the near future. To quote Charles Stuart, 'As soon as you acquire an aircraft like the Dash 7 you are in the big league — even if it's only the fourth division. You can't stay where you are: either you go up — or you go out. I think Brymon will "gain promotion next season" '.

Percival's Provosts

Percival Aircraft has provided the RAF's basic flying training aircraft since just after the war. The three-seat Prentice which served between 1947 and 1955 was the first and least successful of these. The company realised the shortcomings of this underpowered machine and speculatively designed a replacement. This was put forward to the Air Ministry and resulted in the official specification T16/48 being issued. The Percival P56 and Handley Page (Reading) HPR2 were constructed for evaluation, both being powered by the Armstrong Siddeley Cheetah 17 engine, and were all metal, low wing, fixed undercarriage two-seaters of sturdy construction. A year after the first flight of Percival's prototype (which flew on 23 February 1950), the Provost, as it became known,was awarded a production contract for 200 machines to replace the Prentice.

Production Provosts (WV423, WV427 and WV429), powered by the 550hp Alvis Leonides 126 engine, were delivered to the Central Flying School in April 1953 and before the end of the year had replaced Prentices at No 6 FTS Ternhill and No 22 (later No 1) FTS at Syerston. The last of 387 Provosts (XF914) was taken on charge by the RAF on 29 March 1956, by which time it had re-equipped Nos 2, 3, 7 and 8 FTS, the RAF College Cranwell and numerous other training units. Provosts were also supplied to Burma, Eire, Malaysia, Rhodesia and Sudan, some of these being armed versions carrying two .303in machine guns and racks for bombs or 60lb rockets. Provost production totalled 461 aircraft; the last trainer being delivered to the Irish Air Corps on 13 April 1960, just over 10 years after the first flight of the prototype P56. It did not, however, remain in RAF service as a basic trainer for a long period. The manufacturers had the foresight to see the prospects for a pure jet trainer. The design of this new aircraft was based on the development of the Armstrong Siddeley Adder short life

Below:
The stalky undercarriage of the Jet Provost T1 prototype XD674 is a distinctive feature. *Peter R. March*

Right:
The structural similarities of the 'Provost Pair' can readily be seen as Jet Provost T52 G-PROV and Provost T1 G-AWPH fly together. *Peter R. March*

33
G-AWPH
G-PROV

target aircraft jet engine, which became better known as the Viper engine. The structure made use of the Provost's wing, suitably modified, tail surfaces and canopy but with a new fuselage and retractable tricycle undercarriage.

The prototype Jet Provost (XD674), as it was appropriately named, was first flown from Luton on 26 June 1954. A month prior to this the company changed its name to Hunting Percival Aircraft. Ministry interest was immediate and 11 Jet Provost T1s were ordered for evaluation. Trials on this new jet trainer at A&AEE Boscombe Down proceeded satisfactorily, changes being recommended in providing a better clear view canopy and also for the undercarriage to have shorter legs to improve field performance. These improvements were incorporated in the last T1 (XD694) to be produced, being re-designated Jet Provost T2. Service trials began at the Central Flying School, Little Rissington, where the Jet

Above left:
Prototype P56 Provost T1 WG503. *Percival Aircraft*

Left and below left:
A Provost T1 in the markings of No 3FTS RAF Feltwell where it served in 1957-58. *Andrew March*

Bottom left:
The first Jet Provost T1 XD674. *Percival Aircraft*

Above:
Jet Provost T4 operated by the Central Flying School at RAF Little Rissington. *Peter R. March*

Above right:
John Bradshaw flying his Provost T1 G-AWPH, in which he won the Kings Cup Air Race in 1971. *Peter R. March*

Right:
Former Singapore Air Force Jet Provost T52 G-JETP after restoration in 1985. *Andrew March*

Below:
The 'Provost Pair' display team — Mike Carlton flying Jet Provost T52 G-PROV and John Bradshaw in Provost T1 G-AWPH. *Peter R. March*

Top:
A landing Jet Provost T5A . . .

Above:
. . . and a Provost T1 both in the colours of the RAF College, Cranwell. *Peter R. March*

Provost was prepared to become the world's first jet trainer. This was followed by the delivery of six Jet Provost T1s to No 2 Flying Training School at RAF Hullavington in August 1955 to train the first 18 pilots. By 1958 the trials had been completed and it showed that basic jet training was practical.

The Jet Provost was adopted by the RAF as its basic trainer and first deliveries of the production Jet Provost T3 commenced in June 1959. It was followed by the higher powered T4 in November 1961. A further development, the BAC Jet Provost T5, featured a pressurised cockpit, longer nose and a 2,500lb st Viper 201 engine. The Jet Provost T3 remains in service today with the CFS, and Nos 1 and 7 FTS; the T4 has long since been retired from use as a trainer, but a handful soldier on with the CATCS at Shawbury and No 1 TWU at Brawdy. The Jet Provost T5 is operated by Nos 1, 3, 6 and 7 Flying Training Schools, the CFS and the RAF College Cranwell. It is scheduled to be replaced by the Short Tucano shortly. Thus will end a period of some 30 years when Percival's Provosts have been the RAF's most important training aeroplanes.

Waco

Paul McConnell flies a 50-year-old Waco UKC-S biplane from White Waltham airfield. He gives the background to this unique NC15214.

The Waco story begins in the early 1920s when two amateur aeroplane constructors, Clayton Brukner and Elwood Junkin, set up shop to take advantage of the anticipated demand for trainers as the population of war surplus Jennies (the Curtiss JN-4D) dwindled. Establishing themselves in Lorain, Ohio, they took on a noted barnstormer as partner and, to capitalise on his fame, named their venture after him: the Weaver Airplane Co, soon shortened to WACO (pronounced wah-co or whoc-ko, not way-co). By 1923 Brukner and Junkin, now in Troy, Ohio, and bereft of their eponymous partner, had come up with the Waco Seven. This three seat biplane design was sufficiently successful to account, in all its progressively improved variants up to the Waco Ten, for the bulk of the company's production up to 1928. The famous Taperwing appeared in 1929, and by the end of that year Waco had become by far the largest manufacturer of light aircraft in the US.

Amid a prolific flow of new models in subsequent years, the company took the novel step of developing an enclosed cabin aircraft seating four — 'An all-weather airplane with open-model performance' — as the contemporary sales blurb described it. This was rolled out in February 1931, nearly two years before the Beech Staggerwing, and the new aircraft was an immediate hit. The QDC, as it was called, comprised 37 of the 186 Waco aeroplanes sold in 1931. The design was refined considerably for 1932, and in each subsequent year improvements continued. In 1935 a new 'Custom' cabin series was introduced, and to distinguish the existing line the suffix S (for 'Standard' series) was added. In that year most Waco cabins were manufactured with the 225hp Jacobs engine (denoted by the Y prefix) but six Continental-powered UKC-S versions were built as well. The last of these, NC15214, was registered on 8 August 1935 to the Haynes Drilling Co of Tulsa, Oklahoma. List price was $6,285.

NC15214 stayed with its original purchasers until 24 August 1937 and thereafter passed through the hands of owners in a total of 11 states. Initially used by a series of Mississippi air services (and staying with one from 1943 through to 1951), the aircraft passed through a long progression of short term owners culminating in a 12-year period of storage. A Florida restorer found the Waco in New Hampshire in August 1978, and after a

Below:
The colourful Waco retains its former US 'Sunbird' paint scheme. *Peter R. March*

NC
15214

THE SUNFLOWER SEED CO.
NC
15214

Above left:
Cliff Lovell landing the Waco at Shotteswell, soon after he had imported it. *Peter R. March*

Left:
By any standard the Waco is a big, impressive bi-plane. *Peter R. March*

Above:
Paul McConnell flying NC15214 near Reading in March 1985. *Peter R. March*

six-month rebuild it emerged in its present condition. The aircraft was imported into the UK by Cliff Lovell during the summer of 1983. Its current owner (the 19th) operates the Waco from White Waltham airfield in Berkshire. Airframe hours currently total 3,350.

Like its brethren, the chunky UKC-S exemplified a design philosophy which placed function above elegance. The chrome-moly steel tube fuselage structure was built with rugged use in mind, and quality and strength were heavily stressed in the Waco sales pitch. Throughout its existence (the company did not long outlive World War 2) Waco stuck with wooden wings in a biplane format for reasons of lightness and strength. Obtaining greater speed and payload was a matter of using a larger engine, whilst the biplane layout guaranteed the short field performance for which Wacos were famous.

NC15214's low-time Continental R-670 220hp radial pulls it along at a steady 100mph, consuming 10gal/hr at 1,700rpm. The vintage car interior of the aircraft is quite roomy by modern standards but rather noisy as well. Usable passenger/baggage load is nearly 700lb. With a four hour endurance, the Waco's touring capability is excellent, as is its ability to get into and out of small grass airfields. Once airborne, handling is gentle and forgiving, with the stall coming at only 42mph. Like many of its contemporaries, however, the slab-sided Waco can be a real handful in a crosswind, and demands full attention at all times during taxying. Two long-standing and useful modifications to NC15214 are electric starting and hydraulic brakes — original equipment was the Heywood air starter and Johnson Bar brakes. While Wacos of all types are still relatively abundant in the US, NC15214 is the only one in the UK and possibly Europe.

WA669

Bryan Philpott

Meteor Musings

Ever since Flying Officer T. D. 'Dixie' Dean of No 616 Squadron RAuxAF, used the wing-tip of his Meteor F1 EE216 to down a V1 pilotless missile on 4 August 1944, thus recording the first aerial victory of a British designed and built jet-fighter, the stories surrounding the design, development and service of this Gloster thoroughbred have grown. But how much of it is legend? Was the Meteor the classic aircraft that some would have us believe? Was it a dream to fly or a killer? Could it have been sold in greater numbers if refinements had been included at an early stage?

These and many other questions can be answered to a greater or lesser degree by examining contemporary records and talking with those involved. The conclusions reached inevitably will be influenced strongly by personal feelings, or taking certain aspects out of context. Perhaps it is worthwhile looking at some of the broader aspects raised and leaving readers to form their own conclusions, or perhaps be encouraged to look into the subject matter more deeply before deciding into which category he or she, will place the dear old 'Meatbox'.

To settle one of the oldest misconceptions first, the Meteor was designed by George Carter. It is surprising how many people, when posed with the question: 'Who designed Britain's first jet fighter?' answer: 'Frank Whittle'. Whittle of course was responsible for the design of the jet engine, but oddly enough it was a version of his engine designed by Major Frank Halford of de Havillands, that took the prototype (DG206) F9/40 into the air for the first time on 5 March 1943, with Michael Daunt at the controls. The reason for this is that the Whittle engines destined for the first aircraft DG202, were dogged by trouble during manufacture by Rovers, and could not produce the power necessary for flight. This was no reflection on Whittle but a very sorry tale of bungling and maladministration which is another story.

The flight took place from Cranwell, which is appropriate in many ways, not the least being that test pilot, Michael Daunt, was a graduate of the college. Daunt, in this writer's view, has never received the credit due to him for the sterling work he did in flight testing early jet aircraft. He was a contemporary of Douglas

Below:
The record breaking Meteor T7 WA669 at Tangmere prior to the successful attempt on 7 September 1946.
Peter R. March

Bader and flew in the same aerobatic team as the legendary ace at one of the Hendon Air Pageants. Like Bader he too was a first-class rugby player and came close to playing for his native Ireland. His involvement with the Meteor came with the untimely death of Gerry Sayer in a No 1 Sqn Typhoon; but Sayer, who had carried out all the early flying in the single-engined E28/39 and taxying trials in the F9/40, had ensured that Daunt knew all there was to know about jet aeroplanes, which at that time was very little!

Just prior to the first flight of the F9/40, Daunt had suffered minor injuries when he was sucked into the intake of an aircraft that was being ground run, so Glosters very nearly lost two test pilots in a very short space of time. Daunt is still proud of the fact that he was the third object to be sucked into a running engine, the first two being a hat and a tea tray. Such is the humour of the man. It is also interesting and illustrates a typically British bureaucratic situation to recount two more of Daunt's stories relating to the Meteor. On one occasion he was stopped from carrying out test flights at Newmarket Heath, as it was a race day! This, in the middle of a war in which it was hoped that the revolutionary jet fighter would soon be sweeping the enemy from the skies. The other time was during a long and very complicated series of meetings at which certain civil servants were trying to find a new airfield with a long concrete runway where the new fighter could be test flown without hindrance. One venue was selected but rejected because the security risk due to the presence of Irish labourers was considered to be too high. At this point Daunt pointed out that they might just as well abandon the Meteor. In answer to astonished questions, he replied, 'Well, I'm the test pilot and I'm Irish!'

Carter's original brief was for a six gun fighter. Although in his first designs he incorporated six cannons, these were reduced to the familiar four, though production drawings for the Meteor up to the F4 still show the six gun mountings. The central mounting of the 20mm cannons in the aircraft's nose, two either side of the cockpit, gave a concentration of fire that was lacking in the conventionally armed aircraft with wing-mounted weapons, but early problems with ejection of links led to many stoppages and brought about Flying Officer Dean's compromise of tipping his adversary with his wing tip when his guns jammed.

The guns were fed from ammunition tanks located aft of the cockpit, and behind these were the fuel tanks. Like most early jet fighters the Meteor suffered from short duration caused by

Above:
Preserved at Hendon, the Meteor has a plaque on its nose recording the historic event in 1946. *Peter R. March*

Top:
Meteor F4 EE519 carrying two 90lb bombs underwing, on a test flight from Moreton Valence. *Russell Adams*

Right:
One of 65 F4s used by the Royal Netherlands Air Force. This aircraft was previously VW313 with the RAF.

I
75

high fuel consumption, a problem that faced subsequent designs like the Hunter, Swift and Lightning, and was never really resolved until in-flight refuelling was perfected. The Meteor of course played its part in this, and in fact No 245 Squadron was the first operational RAF fighter squadron to be equipped with fighters able to refuel in flight, these being F4s and F8s modified by Flight Refuelling Ltd. They operated out of Horsham St Faith near Norwich, and could be refuelled from RAF Lincoln and American B-29 tanker aircraft. These were the only Meteors to be fitted with fuelling probes which extended from the nose. One record among the many that went to the Meteor, was that set up by F3 EE397 when it stayed airborne for 12hr 3min on 7 August 1949, the pilot being Pat Hornridge of Flight Refuelling, and on this occasion the tanker was a Lancaster.

By the end of the war the Meteor had served in Belgium, Holland and occupied Germany, but had not met the German jets in aerial combat,

Above:
Sqn Ldr Bill Aston leaving Meteor EE387 after making what is believed to be the first landing by an RAF pilot on a carrier (HMS *Illustrious*) at sea, on 14 June 1951.
Via Bill Aston

Below:
Some T7s with F8 tails were dubbed T7, but there is no record what the A&AEE called this T7 with a PR10 nose.
R. Deacon

Bottom:
This Meteor U21A drone of the RAAF was formerly WK798 and served in Korea with No 77 Squadron.
Alain Pelletier

which perhaps was just as well because the Me262 was faster and better armed. It had, however, destroyed 13 V1s, and been highly successful in the ground attack role. Also it proved reliable and rugged which augured well for the future. But its war record, accumulated by just 30 aircraft, was not the straw that broke the Luftwaffe's back, as some would have us believe. Post war, records were there for the taking, and the imagination of the public was captured on 7 November 1945 when Eric Greenwood and Group Captain Hugh Wilson attacked the world air speed record, then held by Fritz Wendel at 468mph in a Messerschmitt Bf109R.

Both pilots succeeded in breaking this by a considerable margin. At first it was thought that the Gloster pilot had obtained the higher average of two runs, but checking the timing equipment proved that it was the Group Captain whose aircraft (EE454 named *Britannia*) had averaged 606mph against Greenwood's 603mph. Incidentally, the RAF pilot's Meteor carried standard service camouflage whereas the mount of Greenwood was overall yellow, leading to the unofficial nickname the 'Yellow Peril'.

Always conscious that the Americans were keen to attack the record and were preparing a P80 Shooting Star to do so, it was decided to make another attempt in 1946 and push the speed well beyond the capability of the American jet.

In July 1946, the RAF established a special High Speed Flight and it was to the 33 ground crew and three pilots that the responsibility

Below:
The Meteor F8 was built in the greatest quantity and served with most RAF UK-based fighter squadrons. WH291 was one of the last to be retired from No 79 Squadron of 229 OCU. *Peter R. March*

Bottom:
A Meteor NF13 at Luqa, Malta, during the Suez landings.

for preparing and flying Meteors for the new attempt fell. Based at Tangmere the flight used several aircraft including EE523 which was later sold to France as F-WEPQ, and EE549 which was to become the new record holder and which is now preserved in the Historic Aircraft Collection at St Athan. The three pilots involved were to become household names: Gp Capt E. M. Donaldson, Sqn Ldr W. Waterton and Flt Lt Neville Duke. It was Donaldson who took the record in EE549 at 616mph, whilst Waterton in EE550 achieved 608mph. The new record was set on 7 September 1946 and was watched by a large crowd which gathered along the sea front. Conditions were far from ideal and low temperatures made a great deal of difference to the times achieved. These particular aircraft were known as 'Star Meteors', and were in essence standard service aircraft with armament removed and various other modifications including uprated Derwent 5 engines. However the modifications did not prevent the claim being made that the Meteors were exactly as those then entering service with Fighter Command, and to support this it was proved that they could be returned to operational status in very quick time.

Behind the scenes the Meteor was earning valuable overseas money. Various sales demonstrations coupled with Arctic trials in Canada, tropical trials in Egypt, and extended visits to Australia, were introducing jet flight to foreign air forces. The first overseas customer was Argentina with an order for 100 F4s. This opened the door to Glosters and soon orders were rolling in from Brazil, Israel, Belgium, Holland, Denmark, Australia, Equador and other overseas forces.

On the home front as well as becoming the mainstay of RAF Fighter Command, it was also carrying out valuable research work and giving an insight into many of the problems that were to be encountered with high speed jet flight. The Meteor was basically a design from the days of piston-engined aircraft, so its shortcomings were highlighted as more powerful engines were fitted and the performance envelope expanded. It is in this respect that many lessons were learned, and it seems odd that a lot of them were not incorporated into the design. This was through no fault of Glosters but, as has been the case throughout aviation history, through interference from government departments and tight purse strings.

An early example was the initial indifference shown to the two seat trainer. Many of the overseas contracts then being won by Glosters involved the training of pilots belonging to the air forces concerned. This was accomplished by an instructor sitting astride the fuselage behind

Below:
A quartet of Meteor NF14s of No 85 Squadron.
Via Ian White

the cockpit and shouting instructions into the trainees' ears. This was not a particularly satisfactory way of overcoming the step from piston to jet engined flight, especially because when it came to flying, the pilot was very much on his own. To obviate this shortcoming Glosters took the wreckage of their demonstration F4 G-AIDC and converted it into a two-seat trainer. In this guise it was registered G-AKPK and was soon acclaimed as a great success. It was only then that official interest became apparent and the Air Ministry issued specification T1/47 for a service version. No doubt official money would have been forthcoming but how long this would have taken if the Company had not had the courage of its convictions to produce the trainer as a private venture, must remain conjecture.

The T7 highlighted one of the handling problems that is often associated with the Meteor, but was in fact only common to the T7. This was a phenomenon known as the 'Phantom Dive'. The most usual place for this to occur was towards the end of the downwind leg, and although it could be encountered in other places the cause was always the same: a total loss of directional control. If the side view of the aircraft is studied it will be seen that the addition of the larger canopy has brought the centre of lateral area much farther forward than in the single seaters. This is exacerbated when a ventral tank is fitted. Directional stability is maintained because the fin is a much better lifting surface at small angles of attack than the fuselage side surfaces. Anything affecting the effectiveness of the fin will reduce directional stability and inducing of yaw could easily lead to loss in directional control. Two of the surest ways of reducing fin effectiveness are flying at high angles of attack, causing fin blanketing, and selecting airbrakes out, thereby creating turbulent airflow over the fin. With the gear down, side area was even further increased, and at high angles of attack with gear and airbrakes extended the airflow turbulence spreads higher up the fin. A typical situation could occur with the T7 on the downwind leg at 1,000ft and 170kt, with flaps up but airbrakes out, speed will have decayed to about 150kt with control becoming less. At this point the undercarriage is selected down. On all Meteors the port wheel lowers first so the pilot has to be ready to counter the slight yaw. If this doesn't take place, the fin can generate little lift to oppose the yaw and, as the forward side surfaces take over, the fin stalls. The increasing

Below:
One of the long-serving Meteor NF11s used by the French Air Force test centre at Mont de Marsan. *Alain Pelletier*

Bottom:
Three of the nine T7s that were supplied to the RDAF, along with 20 F4s, F8s and NF11s. *Gloster Aircraft*

Above:
The most powerful Meteor was WA820 fitted with Armstrong Siddeley Sapphire engines.
Armstrong Siddeley

yaw induces a powerful roll to the left, the nose drops and a 'Phantom Dive' results. The only thing to stop it at this height is the ground. Several students and experienced pilots were killed as a result of this, and it was always something that Meteor pilots had to be wary about. It took about 3,000ft to recover from a deliberately induced 'PD' when it was demonstrated. The best method of recovery was to roll into a spiral, select airbrakes in, undercarriage up, and then take normal dive recovery action. Such was the dread of this situation that it quickly became attributed to all Meteors, and every unexplained crash or dive, was attributed to the 'PD'.

Other Meteors did of course have handling problems, the most common being with ailerons. It took a long time and many different methods of construction and rigging to solve the problem. At one stage it was so serious with the F8 that there were severe doubts as to whether or not the aircraft was safe for the average service pilot. So the Meteor was not a classic in the handling sense, although once mastered it gave few problems to those who had taken the trouble to learn about its faults and how to counter them. Most pilots who operated Meteors have a soft spot for the aircraft, and those who flew several variants will often favour the PR9 or the NF series as being their favourites. The former had the long span wings, and without armament was lighter than the F8. It handled extremely well, had a good all round performance and was very good at its job. It is perhaps in the latter that the secret of the Meteor is answered, for there can be little doubt that by the time the F4 began to be phased out in favour of the F8, the aircraft was well past its prime as an interceptor. The Australians found this to their cost in the Korean conflict when No 77 Squadron discovered its F8s to be no match for the MiG-15 in air-to-air combat, but excellent in the ground attack role. This was a legacy from the days of World War 2, and one that had been foreseen by the Gloster design team, who had proposed such a version, and in fact went as far as producing another PV in the form of the REAPER to support their case.

Design proposals at the time indicate that the company saw a great future for the aircraft in this interceptor role, and studies indicated that wing-tip tanks, a thinner wing, more powerful engines, and modified internal systems would make the Meteor a much more useful aircraft to the RAF. But they were all turned down by the powers-that-be, and at a time when a greatly improved aircraft could have been entering service, albeit still as a stop-gap for second generation interceptors, the rather dated and pedestrian F8 was put into large scale quantity production. This argument does not, however, stand close examination as far as the night fighter versions are concerned. For whereas pilots enjoyed flying an aircraft like the PR9 that was good at its job, and perhaps felt apprehensive about the F8 as an interceptor, they must have been horrified in the task set for them in the NF11 or 14.

Designed by H. R. Watson and built entirely by Armstrong Whitworth Aviation, the night fighter Meteors were well and truly outdated by the time they went into service in 1951. Although they handled well, they had very poor radar and little chance of catching contemporary bombers. In fact on many exercises the Canberras they were sent to intercept often turned the tables on the Meteor and embarrassed the night fighter crew by getting on to their tail and 'splashing' them with their landing lights. A well handled and navigated NF 11 could hold its own against a Lincoln and in good conditions a Washington was a likely 'kill', but in all other cases the crew might just as well have stayed at home and saved the tax payers' money.

Like all other marks of Meteor, the NF versions were also exported, involved in a variety of experiments, and could have been greatly improved for a marginal increase in expenditure. They were initially fitted with British World War 2 radar whilst TRE developed a new British designed and built set, but this was so long in coming and turned out to be such a dismal failure, that American equipment had to be purchased. With thoughts of the Nimrod AEW3 in mind, has anything changed? A proposal to fit the aircraft with Nene engines and thin wings with tip tanks which would have halved the climb rate and increased the endurance was shelved, as was a proposal to fit 30mm cannons. Consequently the first British jet night fighters were lighter armed than the

Below:
A four-engined Meteor F8. WA982 was fitted with RR Soar engines on the wingtips. *Rolls-Royce*

Bottom:
The unusual prone-pilot Meteor — WK935 was converted by Armstrong Whitworth Aircraft for experimental flying. It is now preserved at Cosford. *AWA*

A quartet of Meteor F8s of No 41 Squadron operating from Biggin Hill. *Russell Adams*

X
WA984
W
WA92
WH480

Luftwaffe's Me262 night fighters had been six years earlier.

One of the most important contributions to aviation research made by the Meteor was in the development of the Martin-Baker ejection seat. This started in 1946 with Meteor F3 EE416 from which the first dummy ejection was made on 24 June. This was followed one month and eleven tests later, by the first live ejection when Bernard Lynch left the aircraft at 8,000ft at a speed of 320mph. Subsequently the Meteor featured in the development of practically every seat designed by Martin-Baker and today WL419, a much modified T7 is still carrying on the work and could well end up being the last Meteor flying. This aircraft currently has an F8 tail unit and a Mk 10L(M) rocket-assisted seat installed.

Another interesting aspect of the Meteor in this context was that the Swedish air force was interested in the NF11 provided it could be fitted with Goblin engines and a SAAB-designed ejection seat. AWA under the guidance of Mr Watson produced such a design, but after a great deal of exchange of letters, modifications to the engine and seat installation, the idea was shelved and Sweden opted for the Venom.

Deck landing trials, experiments in STOL, deflected thrust, rocket assisted take-off, auxiliary rocket engines, prone piloting, blown flaps, and many other experiments, some of which laid the pathway to success for modern designs, all fell to the Meteor. It started its life as an interceptor, and it is still helping to keep the pilots of today's more modern equivalents in trim, for its last duty is as a pilotless drone and shepherd aircraft for radio-controlled targets. Three aircraft, two F8s, now known as U16s, one of which is believed to have served in Korea with No 77 Squadron RAAF (WK800), and a T7, (WA662) are used at RAE Llanbedr, where, flown by civilian pilots, they provide a useful facility in the nearby firing range. There are several privately owned NF11s and T7s flying or being restored to flying condition.

It is likely therefore that the familiar shape of the Meteor will be around for a while to come. It may even be seen in the skies during its 50th year in 1993, but was it a classic? This really depends on how one interprets the word. There will be those who will sing the Meteor's praises, and those who damn it. But whatever category future historians put it into, there can be no escaping the fact that it has made an invaluable contribution to aviation and it will be some time before the words of poet D. W. Holmes become reality:

The Meteor of the ocean air
Shall sweep the clouds no more.

Below:
The RAF's last Meteor T7 WA669, was operated by the 'Vintage Pair' for air displays. *Peter R. March*

Geoffrey P. Jones

Homebuilts – French Style

Some names will for ever be associated with France and that country's sport aviation movement. From Blériot at the start, through the infamy of Henri Mignet and his Pou du Ciels, to Joly and Delemontez' Jodels, the French have always been at the forefront in the homebuilt and sport aeroplane world. There are many more besides who helped to build France's postwar aircraft industry: Claude Piel, Yves Gardan, Roger Druine, Marcel Jurca, Rene Fournier and Pierre Robin to name just a few. New designers and their aircraft are now appearing regularly at the shop window of the French homebuilt aircraft movement held every July at Brienne-le-Chateau and together with the 'classics' they make this gathering unique in Europe's aviation calendar.

Homebuilt aviation in France is administered by the Réseau du Sport de l'Air, which has offices in Paris and an active airfield base at Brienne-le-Chateau, situated at the south end of champagne country, about 110 miles southeast of Paris and close to the town of Troyes. The US-built former NATO airfield at Brienne houses the RSA's museum, a rapidly expanding collection of aircraft ranging from homebuilts and gliders through to larger military transports and jets.

Since the death of Henri Mignet in September 1965 at the age of 71, interest amongst the French homebuilt aircraft community in his philosophies and his particular 'Pou-type' aircraft has grown, partly spurred by his son Pierre, but also thanks to Emilien Croses. Croses, from Maçon near Lyon, first built his own personalised variety of the Pou in 1957,the Croses T-1 Geoland, a single-seater powered by a 65hp Continental engine and incorporating long flaps in the trailing edge of the rear 'wing'

Below:
The Druine Turbulent is perhaps the best known of all the French homebuilt designs. This example has a neat cockpit canopy. *Andrew March*

F-PYFT
CARRE D'AS

F-PYIL
POUSS' POU

to improve performance and controllability. There followed the EC-1-03 Pouplume, a low powered, open cockpit motor glider and in 1964/65 his most successful and popular design to date, the EC-6 Criquet. There are now in excess of 25 examples of this unusual but totally practical Pou flying in France and many of these gathered at Brienne in 1984 for the celebrations to mark the 50th anniversary of the publication of Mignet's book on the Pou, 'Le Sport de l'Air'.

Many other homebuilders in France are now building Pou variants, Gilbert Landray with three designs to his credit, Francois Lederlin, G. Briffaud, George Roy, Alain Noel and in the ultralight/microlight category Dominique Lascauds. Examples of Henri Mignet's original designs also continue to be built in the form of the Mignet HM360, HM293 and HM380. These apparently strange machines are proving to be safe and practical aircraft with good performance and seating for up to three people.

It was the Pou du Ciel that started the famous French aviator and designer, Edouard Joly, of Jodel fame, on the road of homebuilt aircraft. Stimulated by the Pou 'fever' sweeping France in 1934/35 he built an HM14 and took it along with eight other builders and their various HM14s to an air rally organised by the French magazine *Les Ailes* at Orly airport in October 1935. After the war he teamed up with Jean Delemontez, his father-in-law, and they designed and built the wood and fabric, single seat, cranked wing Jodel D9 Bebe, which fitted with a 25hp Poinsard engine and registered F-WEPF, first flew on 21 January 1948. Large numbers and varieties of homebuilt and production aircraft designs have followed from this important prototype such that it is estimated that about 4,000 examples derived from the basic Jodel D9 and two-seat D11 have now been built and flown worldwide, this not including factory-built derivatives in the tri-gear Pierre Robin category.

Homebuilders still fly large numbers of 'new' and not-so-new Jodel D9s and D11s but in recent years this French innovativeness has blossomed in numerous new Jodel derivatives, all still retaining that eternal trade mark, the

Left:
Variations on a theme — the modern flea. In the tradition of Henri Mignet's Pou du Ciel, the modern Croses LC6. *Daniel March*

Below left:
The Landray GL03 Pouss-Pou is a 'pusher' version of the flying flea. *Andrew March*

Below:
One of the long line of Jodel variants, the D92 Bebe. *Peter R. March*

'cranked' wing. Alain Cauchy collaborated with Jean Delemontez in the late 1970s to design the two-seat DC01, which looks like the D11 but has the same basic dimensions as the smaller D9. The prototype F-PYFU has a 1600VW engine which at 3,000rpm gives it a cruise of 85mph and rate of climb of 650fpm. The Tri-gear versions of the basic taildragger Jodels are now quite numerous; Ste Aeronautique Bourguignonne at Gueret has built two SAB/Valladeau D119Ts the first being F-WIUM. At Colmar, M. Knoepfli has given similar treatment to the basic D119, and this made its debut at the 1984 Brienne rally. 1985 saw three new Jodel variants including L. Miettaux's DM92 Bebe Special the first tri-gear version of the single-seat D9 and yet another modified tri-gear D11, this time the three-seat, 100hp Lycoming-powered Dessardins DM01 Ibis that first flew in June 1985, registered F-PZIK. 1984 saw the end of another chapter in the Jodel story with the

Right:
The tiny twin-engined Colomban CriCri attracts a great deal of attention whenever it appears. *Peter R. March*

Below:
Variants of variants are common in France. This Dessardins D01 Ibis is derived from the Jodel D11, and was flown for the first time in June 1985. *Geoffrey P. Jones*

Below right:
Avions Pottier has brought a number of new designs to Brienne, including the four-seat all metal P100TS, which was first flown on 16 October 1980. *Peter R. March*

F-PYIJ brittany ferries
brittany ferries
La Grande-Bretagne et l'Irlande depuis Roscoff et Saint-Malo

death at the age of 86 of Edouard Joly, but with new chapters being continually written as the popularity of this classic homebuilt aeroplane continues.

Jodels are mainly wood and fabric in construction but these materials are alien to another increasingly popular and revered designer/builder, Jean Pottier who is based at Les Mureaux near Paris and specialises in all metal construction for his numerous different homebuilt designs. Still only 40 years of age, Pottier is now marketing plans for a range of six different designs of single-, two-, three- and four-seaters, all with tricycle undercarriages and low, mid and high wings. Most popular seems to be the Pottier P180S which first flew in 1979. Although of metal construction it is claimed to be easy to build and to require approximately 600 hours to complete. Its side by side seating, excellent all round cockpit visibility and conventional 1,830cc JPX Volkswagen conversion engine producing 60hp, gives the P180S a 105mph cruise using only one gallon of fuel per 40 miles. At the 1985 Brienne rally eight different Pottier homebuilts

Above:
The Pottier P80S is an all-metal single-seat homebuilt aircraft, which has been followed by the P180S and two-place P170. *Peter R. March*

Below:
Relatively few Druine D5 Turbis have been built. This example was constructed by Claude Bove at Etampes. *Geoffrey P. Jones*

Bottom:
Piel also has a variety of designs including the CP604 Diamant here in taildragger form. *Andrew March*

Above right:
. . . and the CP605 Super Diamant with a tri-gear, photographed at Brienne in 1985. *Geoffrey P. Jones*

Below right:
The Piel CP801 Zef is a popular design with French homebuilders. *Geoffrey P. Jones*

flew in, out of the 40 now flying in Europe and soon to be joined by some of the 140 Pottiers now under construction.

Jean Pottier is an aeronautical engineer by profession working for Aerospatiale. A colleague at the same factory who has revolutionised the meaning of the twin homebuilt is Mike Colomban whose diminutive single-seat Cri-Cri, the world's smallest twin-engined aeroplane, is being built now in large numbers both in France and the USA. Of metal construction, the boxy fuselage and constant chord wings belie the fact that its performance in the air is outstanding. Being fully aerobatic the Cri-Cri is real seat of the pants flying. With the wings being easily detachable it can be stored in a horsebox-type trailer and towed to and from an airfield. Over 25 have now been registered in France and the first of the type is now appearing in the UK.

Whilst the CP301 Emeraude is the design for which Claude Piel is most commonly remembered, he has designed an incredible number of different types and variants of homebuilt aeroplanes, some of which have been built commercially in France and Britain. However, one of the types that can be seen in increasing numbers at any Brienne rally is his single-seat Piel CP80 Zef, a racing monoplane built usually of wood and generally fitted with a 90hp Continental flat-four engine. A particularly 'hot' CP80 is that built by Jean Noan and features the added innovation of a retractable undercarriage. Noan was a colleague of Claude Piel

until his death in August 1982 and helped considerably with his home built project as he did with so many other builders of CP30s, CP60s, CP70s, CP1320s and most recently of the canard ultralight CP150 Onyx, development and marketing of which is now being undertaken by Piel's son, Jean-Claude at Egletons in Southwest France.

The rediscovery of the ultralight aeroplane is a quest that many builders and designers of homebuilts are working on today. With the advent of lighter, more powerful engines, stronger and simpler construction materials and easier construction methods, the homebuilder has never had it so good. Much of the knowledge acquired from the upsurge of interest in powered hang-gliders has been developed in to a new category of light/homebuilt aeroplanes, particularly in France, this being the microlight (ultralight in the USA) and the ARV/ATL. The Robin ATL is an attempt at a production aircraft to provide cheap and reliable flying for two in a relatively cheap and efficient aeroplane. At the 1985 Brienne rally

Below:
The Quaissard GQ01 Monogast first flew in November 1983 and is powered by a 47hp Volkswagen engine.
Geoffrey P. Jones

Bottom:
This futuristic homebuilt, the Grinvalds Orion, can be constructed from a kit of pre-formed composite parts.
Andrew March

several new designs were displayed hoping to emulate these worthy criteria, the most innovative new design being the Erpals JH03, still at single seat prototype stage but being of wood and composite construction, having a 1600JPX pusher engine, canard wing configuration and tricycle undercarriage — subsequent versions will be two-seaters but with the range of 1,200km at 250km/hr on a full tank of 50 litres. Another new design to appear was the Aviasud Mistral, a side-by-side two-seater, tricycle undercarriage, currently with open cockpit, conventionally positioned engine but with a unique pitch control system similar to the Pou with fixed upper wing and fully pivoting lower wing. Getting really down to basics, and of similar ilk to that classic of the homebuilt world, the American Breezy, was the VW-powered two-seat Humbert Moto du Ciel and first of the breed of modern powered ultralights, the autogyro 'fuselage' with wings, J. P. David's pusher VW-powered Raz Mut, F-PYHX.

The list of French homebuilts that are either unique or of which only a few examples have been built is endless, providing the well-versed recognition expert with many headaches. One such aircraft is the very neat, very conven-

Below:
Latest ATL competitor in France is the canard winged Erpals JH03. *Geoffrey P. Jones*

Bottom:
Avions Lucas L5, an all-metal newcomer in 1984. *Geoffrey P. Jones*

Above:
The tiny Gatard Statoplan AG02 Poussin is dwarfed by the RSA's preserved Lockheed Neptune at Brienne.
Geoffrey P. Jones

tional, not unlike a single-seat Cub, Quaissard GQ01 Monogast, which first flew in 1983. Then 1984 saw the debut of a much larger and more sophisticated homebuilt, the Soyer Barritault SB01 from Baugé; a taildragger with retractable undercarriage and large cockpit with three seats it attracted a great deal of attention but also subsequently served to show that the design, construction and development of a new homebuilt have many difficulties. In September 1984 after 30 hours test flying, with everything looking good and after re-design of the retractable gear, the next flight ended with an engine failure on take-off, and whilst the resultant crash was not serious, the limited resources of the homebuilder meant the project being delayed by over a year.

Avions Lucas from Chalon, a little known design team, has flown three different homebuilts to Brienne in the last few years; the L4; and the tri-gear and taildragger versions of the all metal L5. Designer Grinvalds illustrated another aspect of the homebuilt world when he was killed in 1984 whilst carrying out test flying of his sleek and futuristic pusher four-seater, the G802 Orion. Despite this, his design lives on with the aircraft's composite construction being popular with some builders both in France and in the USA, where the aircraft, in kit form, is being marketed by a firm in Texas.

Yves Chasle has been building aeroplanes for many years and his LMC.1 Sprintair, first flying in 1975, is being built by several others in France. Albert Gatard has built several aircraft with a unique system of full span slotted aileron/flaps with adjustments to the tailplane to maintain pitching equilibrium. The full-depth perspex covering of both doors of the very professional looking, all metal Bredelot-Gros BG01 provide this aircraft's distinguishing feature and as well as new designs many French homebuilders concentrate their efforts on rebuilds and restorations of vintage and veteran machines.

The French have always been renowned for their individuality. The homebuilt aircraft 'industry' of France under the auspices of the RSA is certainly no exception, making it only second in the world to that of the prolific USA. The champagne country of France is a pleasant place to visit, and add to this the annual homebuilt aircraft bonanza of the RSA at Brienne each July and it's a job to keep many European sport aviation enthusiasts away.

T. Malcolm English

Icelandic Coast Guard

Established in 1926, the Landhelgisgaezlan (Icelandic Coast Guard) is primarily a law enforcement and rescue organisation. Its mission is to patrol and police the seas around the island, to protect the territorial waters and fishing rights within Iceland's exclusion zone (EZ). Other responsibilities include assisting those in trouble at sea, and removing hazards to navigation such as mines and dangerous flotsam. In addition, the Icelandic Coast Guard provides an emergency ambulance service and maintenance of lighthouse and other navigational aids which might, if malfunctioning, endanger mariners. To fulfil these responsibilities the Coast Guard commands three ships and three patrol aircraft. Its complement of cutters is the *Tyr*, *Aegir* and *Odinn* of 1,300, 1,200 and 1,000 tons displacement, respectively. They are all equipped with hangar and helicopter facilities and are armed with a single 57mm gun.

By the very nature of the vast EZ area around the island and the island's inhospitable terrain, air support is essential. During winter, for example, many of the island's roads are inaccessible. This air support is provided by a Fokker F27 Mk 200 Maritime (TF-SYN) patrol aircraft, an Aerospatiale SA365N Dauphin 2 (TF-SIF) and a Hughes 500D (TF-GRO). The aircraft, as the cutters, are affectionately named after Nordic gods. Ninety per cent of the missions are related to fishery protection with other sorties being flown 'on demand'. Fishery protection missions around the 200-mile EZ are flown by the Fokker F27, which, with its external fuel tanks containing 3,000lb of fuel has an endurance of some 10¼ hours. This

Below:
Dauphin 2 over a beach on the northwest coast of Iceland.
All photographs T. Malcolm English

Above:
Hughes 500D TF-GRO in front of the Coast Guard hangar at Reykjavik.

provides a comfortable margin over the average sortie time of five hours; although flights of up to nine hours have occasionally been necessary. In addition to the 200-mile EZ, there are also often areas within it which are closed to fishing. These are usually monitored by the Dauphin 2.

Operating around the EZ,the F27 has occasionally had to return to Reykjavik to refuel. On these occasions additional support has usually been provided by the Beechcraft King Air belonging to the Icelandic Director of Civil Aviation. This is also hired when the F27 is undergoing its regular maintenance checks. Although the F27 was not initially designed or intended for consistent low level flying, it has proved itself to be an excellent aircraft for the task, both aerodynamically and structurally. Even when low cloud forces operations below the normal height of 1,000-2,000ft, it is remarkably stable and comfortable.

Whilst being delighted with the F27's performance, the Coast Guard is considering updating its systems. Equipment being considered for the retrofit includes a forward looking infra-red system and a searchlight. At the present time,the F27 has a small light in the tail section, but this is considered inadequate for fishery protection sorties at night. Whilst there is a pylon-mounted searchlight on the market, fitment of one may have embarrassing repercussions. Ships also have rather powerful lights and could use them as a weapon against the low and slow F27.

Apart from major inspections and maintenance, which is performed by Icelandair, who also operate out of Reykjavik, all the aircraft are serviced by Coast Guard engineers. The high aircraft availability is a tribute to these staff who work all year round in an inhospitable, unheated hangar.

The Coast Guard's latest aquisition is an Aerospatiale Dauphin 2. Currently under lease from Aerospatiale,it was procured to replace the Sikorsky S76 which was lost in a fatal accident during 1984. The Dauphin 2's chief role is search and rescue, being unique in that all previous helicopters operated by the Coast Guards have been primarily tasked with maritime surveillance. Equipment fitted specifically for the SAR role comprises a Teledyne LORAN C navigation system, Bendix radar, HF radio, emergency flotation gear and a hoist. In rescue operations from ships at sea, the Dauphin 2 uses its 90m long, 272kg capacity winch rather than alighting on the deck. The Coast Guard's cutters are only of some 1,000 tons displacement with small, helicopter landing platforms. Consequently, there are no immediate plans to train crews in operations from such vessels. They do, however, regularly practice lowering and recovering litters from small fishing boats.

The smallest aircraft in the Coast Guard fleet is the float-equipped, four-seat, Hughes 500D. Unlike the Dauphin 2, this is frequently flown from cutters and from late May onwards, is used to service the three Icelandic lightships stationed off the island. This is in addition to its current role of transporting construction materials, as underslung loads, and providing maintenance support to the island's lighthouses and other navigation aids. Another of its frequent tasks is in ferrying surveyors to areas inaccessible by road, usually in the mountainous regions.

The Coast Guard works closely with several Icelandic life-saving organisations and the USAF's Detachment 14 of the 67th Air Rescue and Recovery Squadron, which is based at Keflavik and has compiled a programme for such groups in order to educate them in how to operate with their helicopters. This is of particular importance to the 'amateur' organisations who, whilst doing stirling service, have

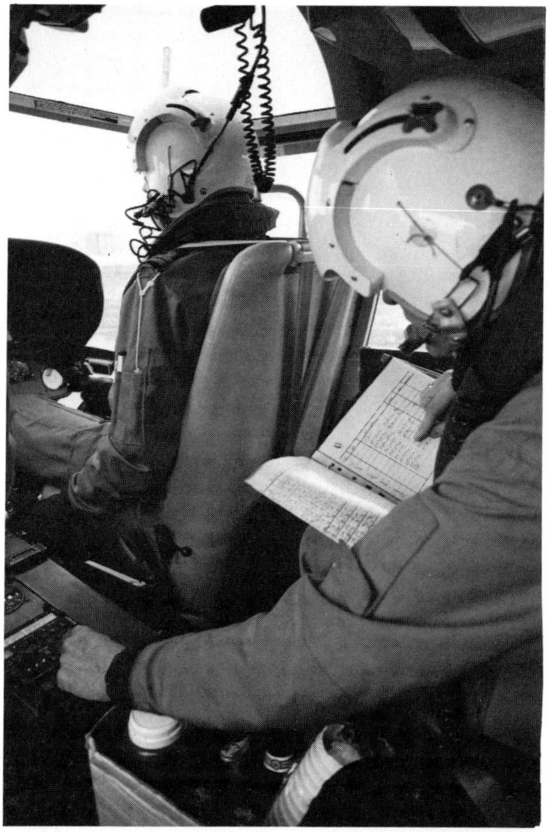

Left:
Keying in waypoints to the Dauphin's LORAN C navigation system.

Above:
Sigurdur St Ketilsson using a BAe (Stevenage) Steadyscope during a fishery protection sortie.

Below:
Cabin interior of the Fokker F-27.

little idea of helicopter operational requirements. These courses feature rescue film and slide shows, but more importantly, subject attendees to working in helicopter downwash. They are given experience of being winched and they are also instructed in how to strap patients

into a litter, choose a suitable landing site and illuminate a site for night operations.

Because of the Dauphin 2's limited 150-mile radius of operation, the Coast Guard relies heavily on the long range capability of Det 14's HH-3E rescue helicopters for many of the emergency missions at sea. In general, there is a good working relationship with Det 14 but in a recent operation, involving all of the rescue organisations on the island, there was an obvious lack of liaison which suggests the need for a co-ordinating authority.

Above:
Fokker F-27 Mk 200 Maritime in the Coast Guard hangar at Reykjavik.

Below:
The Coast Guard's three cutters in Reykjavik harbour.

In spite of the reduction in the amount of illegal fishing since the 1975 'Cod War', the Coast Guard is an extremely busy unit and if a proposal by the Icelandic Minister for Foreign Affairs is approved, the work-load may increase still further. He has suggested that it 'ought to perform an active part in the military surveillance work around Iceland'.

John Dunnell

'Tiger' Squadron

The introduction of the F-4J Phantom F-3 into RAF service in 1984 was an event made doubly significant as the unit chosen for this task was the re-formed No 74 'Tiger' Squadron. The return of the 'Tigers' to the RAF's front line was welcomed by enthusiasts inside and outside the service, for this squadron, perhaps more than any other, has been associated with many of the significant developments in the postwar jet age air force. No 74's nickname was gained during World War 1, when from inauspicious beginnings as a training squadron formed in July 1917, No 74 went on to play an effective part in the final offensive leading to Germany's defeat. Taking its SE5As to France in March 1918 the squadron was mostly involved with offensive patrols, carrying 25lb bombs for targets of opportunity. Before the end of May, 74's pilots had destroyed 70 enemy aircraft and were acquitting themselves equally well in their strafing role. By the armistice the squadron's tally had doubled to 140 and the reputation of its pilots was second to none. Nevertheless, after a short period in Germany the squadron was returned to England in February 1919 and disbanded in July.

The Abyssinian crisis of 1935 resulted in 74 Squadron being reformed, equipped with Hawker Demons. It was intended to form 74 from a flight of No 23 Squadron on 1 September 1935. At the time No 23 was en route to Malta by troopship so 74's effective re-birth had to await its arrival at Hal Far. The squadron's job here was to provide local air defence for Malta against anticipated Italian air attacks. Had this crisis not arisen No 74 would have re-formed at a later date as a home defence unit, and indeed the squadron returned to the UK in July 1936, bringing its Demons to Hornchurch in Essex.

April 1937 saw the Demons replaced by Gloster Gauntlet single-seat fighters, the first aircraft to carry the squadron's colourful tiger skin markings. Alongside Nos 54 and 65 squadrons, No 74 comprised the Hornchurch Wing. The following years were a period

Below:
Unloading a No 74 (F) Squadron Demon from SS *Maihar* in Grand Harbour Valetta, Malta, in September 1935.
All photographs via No 74 Squadron unless otherwise credited

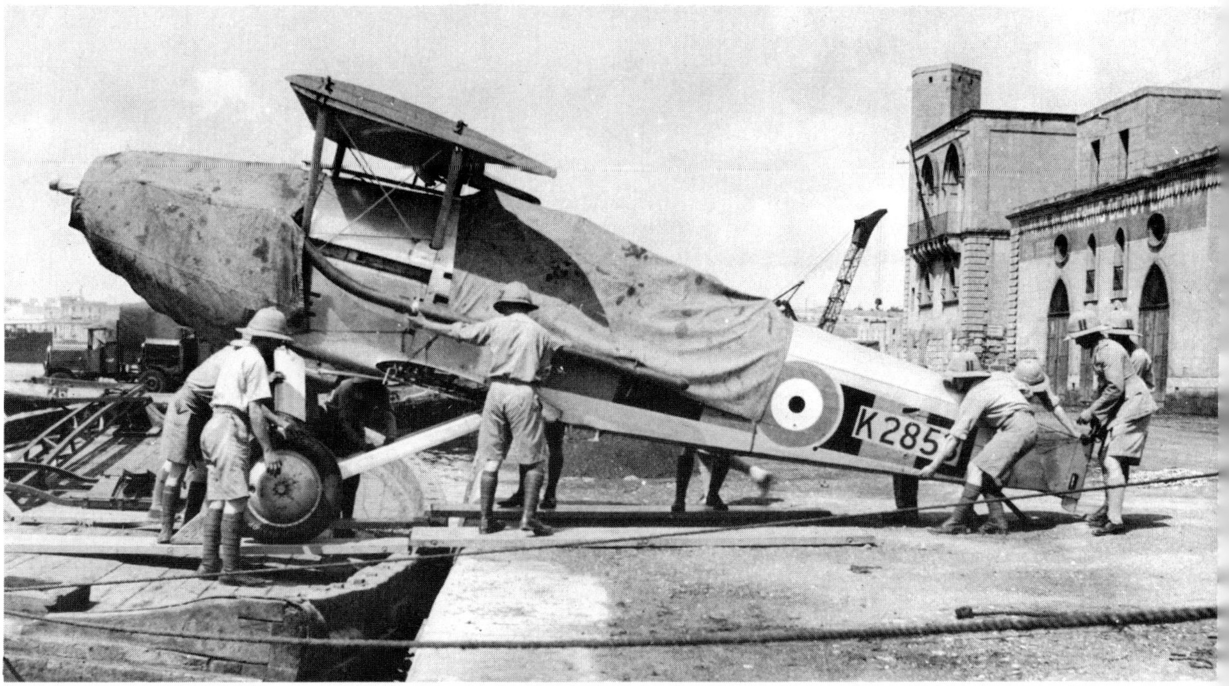

4D

Left:
Engine change on a Gauntlet at Hornchurch in 1937. The squadron's tiger stripes can be seen on the rear fuselage.

Above:
74's pilots with Meteor F3 EE341 at Colerne after the squadron formed part of the RAF's first jet fighter wing.

Below:
Spitfire LFXVI with 500lb bombs on underwing racks at Drope, Germany in May 1945. It was being flown by the squadron's CO Sqn Ldr Reeves.

of re-equipment for Fighter Command, and as war in Europe loomed there was much controversy surrounding the choice of tactics to be used by the expanding home defence force. During the 1938 contest for the Sir Philip Sassoon Trophy for fighter combat tactics, No 74 Squadron's team was led by one of its Flight Commanders, Flying Officer A. G. 'Sailor' Malan. In spite of flying the most outdated entrant, Malan's flight won the trophy by ignoring accepted methods and using Malan's own ideas. Malan went on to become one of the RAF's top scoring fighter pilots and it is worth noting that the methods he used reflected the tactical thinking of his famous predecessor in the No 74 Squadron of 1918, Mick Mannock VC.

After the Munich crisis of September 1938 deliveries of the long-awaited Spitfire were accelerated. The Hornchurch Wing re-equipped in the spring of 1939 and this airfield was to be 11 Group's only all-Spitfire sector station throughout the Battle of Britain. This possibly reflects the length of time needed to attain full proficiency on the new fighter. Indeed 74, which had been the first of Hornchurch's squadrons to re-equip, could only just be considered combat-ready by the outbreak of war on 3 September 1939. Three days later flying its second scramble of the war, a section of 74's Spitfires shot down two Hurricanes of No 56 Squadron! This 'Battle of Barking Creek' was sparked off by a failure of the RDF (radar) system which fortunately was never repeated with such tragic results.

11 Group's precious Spitfire squadrons got their first real taste of combat during May 1940 while attempting to protect the Dunkirk

beaches. 74's patrols over France began on 20 May and during one week five of its pilots were lost. The Squadron claimed 19 enemy destroyed, Malan scoring his first victories — a Heinkel 111 and a Junkers 88 — on 21 May. From then until its withdrawal to 12 Group in mid-August, No 74 Squadron was even more heavily engaged with the enemy.

July saw increasing Luftwaffe attacks on convoys and the Channel Ports. For much of the

Above:
With Tiger badges on the nose, a line-up of 74's Meteor F4s at Horsham St Faith for the 1948 air defence exercise Operation 'Dagger'.

Below:
Meteor F8s were delivered during September and October 1950.

Below right:
A quartet of Meteor F8s rehearse for the local 'Battle of Britain at Home' display at Horsham St Faith.

time No 74 Squadron was detached to the forward airfield at Manston in order to reduce the time taken to react to warnings of incoming raids. Frequently the 'Tigers', normally led by Malan, were in action against groups of free ranging Messerschmitt Bf109s. Their greatest problem was to avoid being 'bounced' by the enemy whilst still climbing out of Manston. 74's pilots usually gained the upper hand in these actions, acquitting themselves particularly well in the sharp dogfights which took place on Sunday 28 July against the 109s of JG51 led by Luftwaffe ace Major Werner Molders. Malan himself damaged Molders' 109, the wounded German crashlanding on the French coast. Similar actions continued into August, until Tuesday 12 August, designated 'Adler Tag' (Eagle Day) by the German High Command. The Luftwaffe then turned its attentions to RAF airfields, No 74 being the only squadron to intercept the first wave of Dornier 17s before they penetrated inland in bad weather.

The 'Tigers' were now in desperate need of a respite from the exhaustive action of 11 Group and on 14 August were withdrawn to Wittering. Re-equipped with Spitfire IIs, the squadron was back in action on 9 September, operating from Coltishall as part of 12 Group's 'big wing'. The pitch of operations was now less intense and in October 1940 74 moved to Biggin Hill, with the Battle of Britain all but over. Superbly led by Malan, 74 sought every opportunity for action and in the last two months of 1940 destroyed 38 enemy aircraft.

Moving on to the offensive in 1941 fighter sweeps were flown over France as often as the weather permitted. May saw the arrival of cannon-armed Spitfires, which the squadron relinquished in July when it moved to Acklington with Spitfire IIs again. The 'Tigers' were to see little further action in Europe and even less when, in April 1942, they embarked for Africa without any aircraft! The next two years saw a variety of unspectacular duties including servicing American Liberators and flying oilfield protection sorties with worn-out Hurricanes. For part of this period the squadron was operational again, being driven out of Cos in October 1943 before languishing at various Mediterranean bases.

Returning to the UK in April 1944, 74 was operational with Spitfire IXs in time to play a part in the build up to D-Day. Flying out of Lympne the squadron carried out escort duties with some ground attack sorties in the invasion area itself. Anti-V1 flying bomb duties interrupted this work in July for a brief period until the squadron joined the Second Tactical Air

Above:
Before being replaced by Hunters the squadron's Meteors were camouflaged, although they retained the colourful tiger markings.

Above right:
This formation of Hunter F6s was photographed in 1960, as the squadron was preparing to convert to Lightnings.

Right:
The three jet types operated by No 74 Squadron — Meteor, Hunter and Lightning at Coltishall in September 1960.

Forces' No 145 Wing at Selsey. Rapidly completing a bombing course at Southend the 'Tigers' were chosen to escort a DC-3 carrying Winston Churchill to France on 7 August. The Squadron itself moved to France two weeks later, joining three French squadrons at Sommervieu. Close support and escort missions were now 74's daily routine, with regular moves forward following the Allied advance. Late in September continuous patrols were flown over Arnhem and Nijmegen by the squadrons of 145 Wing before returning to ground-attack work in October.

Losses from enemy action were now light, although poor weather in November and December made life for the squadrons difficult. 145 Wing escaped the Luftwaffe's New Year's Day surprise attack (operation 'Bodenplatte') and as the weather improved the pace of operations again picked up. 74 received Spitfire XVIs in March 1945 but were not happy with their new aircraft. The finish was poor, giving a lower speed than was obtained from the Mk IXs, and the Packard-built engines were prone to oil and coolant leaks. Persevering nevertheless, the squadron flew intensively, moving forward into Germany on 10 April 1945. Towards the end of the month the weather again hampered operations, and 74 Squadron's war ended with them grounded.

Almost immediately 74 returned to England and to Fighter Command, joining Nos 616 and 504 Squadrons at Colerne to become the RAF's first jet fighter wing, with Meteor F3s. After a difficult period working up on the new type the squadron moved to Bentwaters in September 1946, going on to its 'permanent' base at Horsham St Faith the same month. The Horsham Wing began to convert to Meteor F4s in December 1947. The enthusiasm for this change can be imagined as the type had taken the world speed record to 616mph not long before. The 'Tigers' were now an integral part of the UK's air defences once again, regularly participating in major exercises over the East coast. Meteor F8s arrived in 1950, appearing the following year with 74's 'tiger' markings reinstated.

They were so equipped for the next seven years, during which the developments at home and overseas clearly indicated that the Meteor

was becoming obsolete. The 'Tigers' were perhaps fortunate to avoid the trials and tribulations encountered by those squadrons faced with taking the Hawker Hunter F1s and F2s 'into service and into trouble'. Nevertheless, their impatience to be re-equipped could not have been helped by the arrival at Horsham St Faith of a modification centre for Hunter F4s early in 1956. The space demanded by this centre in fact delayed 74's re-equipment for a year and it was from February 1957 that the first Hunter F4s carried the squadron's now famous markings. The further-improved Hunter F6s arrived nine months later, the whole squadron using this type by January 1958. From June 1959 to January 1960, No 74 operated from Coltishall whilst Horsham was resurfaced. Later that year 74 returned permanently to Coltishall in preparation for its greatest peacetime challenge — the introduction of the English Electric Lightning F1 into RAF squadron service.

The Air Fighting Development Squadron at Coltishall had received Lightnings in December 1959 and assisted 74's conversion to its new aircraft in July and August 1960. In spite of the demanding nature of this conversion the 'Tigers' were able to fly a four-ship formation on most days of the Farnborough Air Show in September that year. Pressing on with the task of proving the RAF's first integrated weapons system, the squadron took part in its first exercise with Lightnings in April 1961, achieving an excellent kill rate. By now 74 had been designated a night and all-weather unit, underlining the Lightning's potential. The national press lavished considerable attention on the squadron during this period and the

B

FLT.LT. M.E. BEE
C.T. HUNT
DANGER
KEEP CLEAR OF INTAKE
WHEN ENGINE IS RUNNING

'Tigers' were again in the public eye at Farnborough in 1961, this time with nine aircraft. In 1962 the squadron became the RAF's leading aerobatic team known as 'The Tigers'; each aircraft carrying the tiger's head marking on an all black tail fin. In that year they appeared at Farnborough in formation with Hunters of No 92 Squadron.

74 continued to operate from Coltishall until February 1964 when the squadron moved to Leuchars to re-equip with the much improved Lightning F3 in April. The 'Tigers' were now better located to deal with probing Russian reconnaissance bombers, meeting them well out over the North Sea, using in-flight refuelling as necessary. Their efficiency at this task was increased when the longer range F6 Lightnings were received from August 1966. These followed an intensive period of in-flight refuelling practice, which included a trip by four aircraft to Cyprus in January 1967, with overwing tanks sometimes fitted. All this was preparation for Exercise 'Hydraulic', the transfer of 74 from Leuchars to Tengah on Singapore island.

Thirteen Lightnings had arrived at Tengah by 11 June and were declared operational the following day. For the next four years the 'Tigers' were the Far East Air Force's only air defence squadron, participating in a wide variety of exercises involving the Royal Navy, RAAF, USAF and others. In 1970, aircraft of No 5 Squadron joined 74 in Singapore to participate in local defence exercises. On conclusion, No 5's pilots brought back some of the 'Tiger' aircraft for major overhauls in the UK.

In August 1971, the squadron's tour in the Far East came to an end; the Lightnings were flown to Cyprus and the squadron was

Left:
A Lightning F6 is brought out of the hangar at Tengah, Singapore, in 1968 to commence a day's work.
Peter R. March

Below:
One of 74's Lightning F1As about to take off.
Peter R. March

Above:
In 1960 the squadron displayed four of its Lightnings at Farnborough. *Peter R. March*

Left:
In 1961 'The Tigers' flew a nine Lightning display.

Below:
An F-4J of No 74 Squadron in company with an F-4S of VF301 over Southern California in the summer of 1984.

disbanded. There were many rumours that the 'Tigers' were to be re-formed, last occurring when it was proposed that the Binbrook Lightning wing was to be expanded in 1980. But this was not to be. The squadron's eventual re-appearance in 1984 resulted from the experience of the Falklands War. The need to provide permanent fighter protection for the Islands was met by stationing a Phantom squadron there, and this in turn reduced the UK's already thin air defence cover.

Clearly more Phantoms were needed and the most compatible, readily available type was the ex-US Navy F-4Js, held in store following their replacement by F-14 Tomcats. Fifteen low-hour examples were selected and after a considerable life extension and improvement programme these were delivered to the UK. The first examples arrived at Wattisham in August 1984, their grey colour scheme adorned with 74's distinctive markings. The squadron's task was to bring these somewhat different Phantoms to a state of operational readiness, a job perhaps made more difficult as Wattisham's squadrons concurrently began to transfer to a new hardened environment comprising aircraft shelters, briefing facility and personnel shelters.

The new aircraft differ from the RAF's F-4K

Top:
Phantom F3 high over the North Sea in February 1985 after refuelling from a VC10 tanker. *Peter R. March*

Above:
A well armed F3 on finals to land at Wattisham.
John Dunnell

and -M Phantoms in many respects, the most significant being the engine. The difference in thrust and throttle response between the General Electric J79 engines of the F-4J and the Rolls-Royce Speys fitted to the other RAF Phantoms, combined with the higher frontal area needed to accommodate the Speys, means that the F-4Js have a slightly poorer performance at low level but are significantly better at higher altitude. In terms of equipment, the Westinghouse radar together with its digital computer gives the F-4J an improved capability. The already capable radar warning receiver has also been enhanced. The American weapons mix of Sidewinder and Sparrow is being augmented to include Sky Flash and fuselage-mounted gun pod.

Anyone visiting the 'Tigers' at Wattisham cannot fail to be impressed by the high morale as the squadron continues to build on its tradition as a front line air defence unit, the only survivor of those three original squadrons of the RAF's first jet-equipped wing. There can be no doubt that 74's Phantoms will continue to play a key part in the UK's defences alongside the other Phantom, Lightning and new Tornado F23 units of Strike Command's No 11 Group well into the future.

T. Malcolm English

NASA's ER-2

It was in April 1956 that the first Lockheed U-2 detachment arrived in England, ostensibly for weather research. However, it is now known that the 1st Weather Reconnaissance Squadron, Provisional, formed at RAF Lakenheath, was a front for CIA overflights of the Soviet border. Almost 29 years later on 23 March 1985, a variant of this famous, or infamous, aircraft arrived back in the UK in a genuine civilian role.

The derivative was a Lockheed/NASA ER-2, 80-1063/N706NA (NASA 706), research aircraft. Normally based at the Ames Research Centre, NAS Moffett, California; it was operating out of Mildenhall for atmospheric and geological surveys of the United Kingdom. Not only was this the first visit of the ER-2 to Mildenhall, it was also the only time that the aircraft had operated outside the USA. During its five week deployment the ER-2 flew when the weather permitted, using a multitude of sensors to gather information on the UK environment. Most of the sorties were of at least six hours duration and flown at a height of 65,000ft. Much of the technology used on the ER-2 was developed for the Landsat earth resources satellite programme and included a high-resolution camera and infra-red sensors.

The ER-2 is a 'demilitarised' variant of the Lockheed TR-1A, N706NA being the third aircraft scheduled to be delivered off the TR-1 production line. In the event, however, it was the first off the line, thus effectively becoming the prototype TR-1A. Its first flight was on 11 May 1981. As an aside, the reason why NASA flies the ER-2 with an Air Force serial number, in addition to the civilian one, is that it enables the aircraft to use fuel without having to pay Federal fuel taxes.

As previously mentioned, the ER-2 is basically a TR-1 without that type's military sensor interfaces. Whilst retaining the general appearance of NASA's U-2C, the ER-2 incorporates many new features, increasing its already remarkable performance. The most significant modification is its larger wing with a refined aerofoil section. This provides almost double the payload capacity and a 20-30% improvement in range and endurance. But of even greater importance, at least to the pilots, is its more spacious cockpit. Amongst other things, this has facilitated a Lockheed zero-zero rocket-powered ejection seat. Other changes to the earlier U-2s include the more powerful Pratt & Whitney J75 turbojet engine. The net result of these improvements is a maximum range of more than 3,000 miles, an endurance of some 12hr and an operating ceiling of 90,000ft.

Equipment may be carried either within the

Below:
The ER-2 on approach to land at Mildenhall; note the split flaps fully extended.
All photographs T. Malcolm English

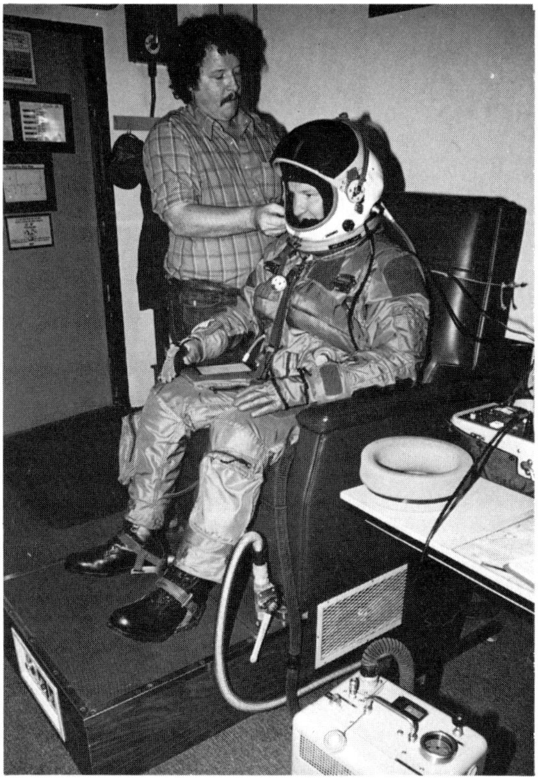

fuselage or in underwing slipper pods, called 'super pods'. There are two main fuselage bays, a pressurised, air conditioned 'Q-bay' and a nose compartment. These are capable of carrying 750lb and 600lb respectively. The 'Q-Bay' is located immediately aft of the cockpit and forward of the engine air intakes. The nose compartment, as its name implies is forward of the cockpit area. The 'super pods' are mounted at about ⅓rd span and are able to accommodate 750lb each. In addition a small number of sensors may be carried in, or on, wing-tip fairings.

Flight at the altitudes typical of ER-2 operations poses problems for both pilot and aircraft. At heights above 10,000ft oxygen support is necessary and above 25,000ft there is a real danger of decompression sickness, more popularly known as the 'bends'. In other military aircraft and airliners, pressurisation is achieved by tapping air from the engine compressor. At 65,000ft, however, the air is mixed with heavy concentrates of ozone and triatomic oxygen, neither of which is compatible with the human breathing system. Furthermore, the air pressure at that height is so low that water boils at 37°C, which is normal body temperature. Without pressurisation a pilot would simply vaporise! In order to survive

Above left:
Pilot Jerry Hoyt is fitted with a full pressure suit.

Above:
Cockpit close-up. Above the control yoke is the drift sight screen.

Above right:
Refuelling with low vapour pressure kerosine.

Right:
The combination of suit and canopy does not give the pilot a very good field of vision.

in such a hostile environment, ER-2 pilots are obliged to wear a full-pressure suit. Suiting-up normally begins more than an hour before entering the aircraft, as the pilot has to breathe 100% oxygen for at least 45 minutes before take-off to prevent the 'bends'. While he does this a fellow pilot carries out internal and external aircraft pre-flight checks.

Primary flying controls are manually operated, with a yoke for the aileron/elevator and pedals for rudder movement, typical 1950s state of the art technology. Aerodynamically, too, the ER-2 is quite conventional, the most noticeable feature being its long span, high aspect ratio wing and tail surfaces. By utilising wing tip plates or sensor fairings, the effective aspect ratio is increased thus reducing lift-induced drag still further. The ER-2's performance and wing design caused a few fuel system problems. For example, at high altitude, low air pressure tends to cause liquids to vaporise, so a special, low-vapour-pressure kerosine is burned, although the J75 is capable of operating with standard fuel. Venting problems due to the aircraft's steep climb angle and high rate of climb, approximately 45° and 8,000ft/min at sea level respectively, were solved by exhausting at the fin tip.

Probably the most significant design achievement, and the secret of the ER-2's amazing performance, is its lightness; the empty weight is a mere 15,500lb. This has been achieved by a considerable amount of hand building and attention to structural and system weight saving. Typical of the innovative features, incorporated to save weight, is its bicycle landing gear with twin-wheel 'pogo' outriggers. With the exception of training sorties, the 'pogos' are jettisoned on take-off. For landing, lateral support may be provided by skids fitted to wing tip plates or sensor pods. Quite often, however, pilots balance their aircraft down to walking pace, until ground crew are able to re-insert the 'pogos'.

The ER-2's conventional glider-like configuration and modest operating speeds may lead one to assume that it has docile handling qualities. Nothing could be farther from the truth. At high altitude, the airspeed has to be held within narrow limits as there may be only 8kt difference between stall speed and the onset of Mach buffet. One U-2 pilot reported that in a turn, at operational height, one wing was sometimes in stall buffet and the other in Mach buffet. Similarly, at high altitudes, turns have

to be made with shallow bank angles, otherwise there is a considerable height loss due to the reduced lift. Autopilot turns are understood to be restricted to 20° of bank.

Even at low altitude the pilot has his hands full. To quote a U-2 pilot 'it handles like a truck in the circuit'. Due to the aircraft's high lift to drag ratio, the threshold speed is critical. Too high and it will float forever. It is also very susceptible to thermals and gusts on final approach. Overshoots are then a problem due to the J75's long acceleration time. Because of the high pilot workload during the landing phase he is assisted in a chase car by a fellow pilot, who calls out descent rate and height above the runway.

All of the information gathered from the ER-2's sorties, be it relating to pollution of the air or soil, or the health of crops, will be made available to the relevant authority. In some cases this may be the owner of a small holding. Considering the Powers' U-2 flight on 1 May 1960, which resulted in Khrushchev walking out of the Paris summit talks later that month, it is almost a classic case of a sword turned into a ploughshare.

Right:
The ER-2's stringer nose construction is revealed through its thin skin.

Below:
The bicycle landing gear and infra-red scanner can be clearly seen in this take-off shot.

Roger Wasley

Wasp Loses its Sting

An important chapter in British naval aviation history is drawing to a close as the last Wasp helicopters are withdrawn from Royal Navy service. The Wasp was the first helicopter designed specifically for operation from small warships and has seen more than 20 years' service with the Navy. It successfully pioneered the special techniques which have added enormously to the capabilities of the Navy's frigates.

The five-seat Wasp shared its heritage with the Scout and originated in November 1957 when Saunders-Roe began a private venture design for a Skeeter replacement. Two Saro P531 prototypes were built and the first (G-APNU) flew on 20 July 1958. The second (G-APNV) made its maiden flight on 30 September and is now displayed at the Fleet Air Arm Museum at Yeovilton as XN332. Both prototypes were powered by Blackburn-Turboméca Turmo 603 shaft turbines, derated to 325shp, and incorporated several Skeeter components, including the tailboom and short-legged tricycle undercarriage.

Following initial evaluation by pilots at A&AEE Boscombe Down, exhaustive naval trials were carried out from November 1959 with the modified G-APNV and two specially-built P531-0/Ns (XN333 and XN334) which had Turmo engines but were fitted with quadricycle undercarriage and landing skids. These trials were conducted by the Navy in conjunction with RAE Bedford to identify, investigate and solve the problems associated with helicopter operations from small ships. They were first carried out on HMS *Undaunted* using a small 21ft by 26ft platform built aft. These were believed to be the first landings by a helicopter on a frigate. The P531s made hundreds of take-offs and landings aboard frigates, by day and night, and 19 different landing gear/deck securing systems were evaluated before a successful formula was derived. Meanwhile, other aids and modifications were being developed, including the glidepath indicator, autopilot and autostabiliser, blade and tailfolding mechanisms and the flotation gear.

Below:
The first Saro P531 prototype G-APNU airborne from Eastleigh in 1958.

The trials having been deemed a success, the P531 was ordered into production as the Sea Scout HAS Mk 1 — this name being changed subsequently to the Wasp. The first of two pre-production Wasps, XS463, built by Westland's Fairey Division at Hayes, first flew from White Waltham on 28 October 1962. The Royal Navy received 96 production Wasps and the first, XS527, flew in January 1963. This aircraft was taken on charge on 6 June 1963 and was eventually withdrawn from service in November 1985, having served with HMS *Endurance* during and after the Falklands conflict.

Production Wasps were powered by the 1,050shp Rolls-Royce Bristol Nimbus 103 turboshaft engine, derated to 710shp. Maximum speed was 120mph, cruise speed 110mph and maximum range 295 miles. The four main rotor blades and the two-bladed tail rotor pylon folded for stowage on ship. The four wheels were fully castoring and were provided with sprag-type brakes. There were two side-by-side seats at the front of the cabin and a bench seat for three at the rear.

A weapon load of 540lb (245kg) could be attached between the undercarriage legs, comprising two Mk 44 or Mk 46 homing torpedos, or an equivalent weight of depth charges or bombs. Wasps could also be equipped with the Nord/Aérospatiale AS12 wire-guided air-to-surface missile system.

The Wasp HAS1 first entered service with No 700W Squadron, the Initial Flying Trials Unit, formed at RNAS Culdrose on 4 June 1963.

Above:
'PNU making its public debut at the SBAC Show in 1958.

Above right:
The second P531 was used for service trials as XN332 and is now in the Fleet Air Arm Museum at Yeovilton.
Roger Wasley

Right:
Full operational evaluation was conducted at RAE Bedford with XN333 and XN334. The latter is shown here with dummy torpedoes. *Roger Wasley*

Below right:
The first production Wasp HAS1 XS527 remained in service for 22 years, being retired in November 1985.
Peter R. March

Its task was to develop the handling techniques and smooth out any technical problems associated with the new helicopter and new concept in anti-submarine warfare. The first Small Ship Flight, for HMS *Leander*, was formed on 11 November.

When the initial trials were completed, 700W Squadron was disbanded on 4 March 1964 and No 829 Squadron was commissioned as the Headquarters squadron to parent all Small Ships Flights and provide operational flying training for Wasp pilots. On 28 May the Wasp made its first major public appearance at the 50th anniversary of the Fleet Air Arm at Yeovilton, when five Wasps took part in the flypast. Then, on 1 December, No 771 Squadron became part of No 829 Squadron and moved to RNAS Portland where the unit has remained

DANGER
XN 332
ROYAL NAVY
759

DANGER
XN334
ROYAL NAVY

DANGER
ROYAL NAVY
434

ever since. Portland was a more logical base, as this allowed the Wasp and ship to work-up together.

15 March 1965 saw the first foreign visit by a Royal Navy Wasp when 'Eskimo' Flight's aircraft flew to RNNS De Kooy in the Netherlands. The first ditching of a Wasp occurred on 7 July and was caused by a lost balance weight on the rotor head. In the light of later experience this ditching might have been avoided, though at the time the pilot, Lt Christmas, received a green endorsement for his handling of an extremely tricky situation at night. The incident had a lighter side, since on

Above:
Air-to-surface wire-guided missiles could be fired from Wasps by day or night. *HMS Osprey*

Below:
A Wasp equipped with Nord AS12 wire-guided missiles working with a fast training boat. *Peter R. March*

Right:
This Wasp from HMS *Endurance* assisted in immobilising the Argentine submarine *Santa Fé* during the Falklands conflict. *Andrew March*

Below right:
No 829 Squadron's XS533 overhead a 'Leander' class frigate HMS *Argonaut*; it is carrying Mk 44 homing torpedoes. *Peter R. March*

hitting the water the pilot found the engine still running and, with rotors engaged, the aircraft started to motor through the water! This caused such a force of water on to the pilot, that he was unable to lean forward and switch off the high pressure fuel cock to stop the engine.

The sinking of the Israeli destroyer *Eilat* in October 1967 by a missile-armed fast patrol boat emphasised the need for the Royal Navy to have a helicopter equipped with air-to-surface missiles. Nord SS11 missile firing trials began in December 1968 and the following February saw the first firing of the improved AS12 from a Wasp. Night firing trials followed in October.

No 829 Squadron's initial complement was three HQ aircraft and four Ships' Flights helicopters, but this number steadily grew and in January 1972 the training of Wasp aircrew was taken up by the newly-formed No 703 Squadron. By the end of 1977, No 829 Squadron had 42 front-line aircraft and 703 had 22 for training. This split lasted for nine years until the squadrons were amalgamated in January 1981.

Wasps were operated from frigates of the 'Leander', 'Tribal' and 'Rothesay' classes, from survey and ice patrol ships, and also from early Type 21 ('Amazon' class) frigates prior to the Lynx entering service. The Wasp was incorporated into the ship from which it operated as an essential part of the vessel's capability. So successful was the concept that it is now almost unthinkable that the Royal Navy would order ASW warships without a helicopter on board.

A Wasp was often carried by the Commando carriers *Bulwark* and *Albion*, being attached to the Wessex squadrons for forward air control and liaison duties. No 706 Squadron at RNAS Culdrose operated six Wasps for training during the 1960s and early 1970s and Britannia Royal Naval College used a Wasp for air experience flights.

Wasps distinguished themselves during active service in the Falklands Crisis of 1982 and helped put the Argentine submarine *Sante Fé* out of the war. Late on 24 April, HMS *Antrim* detected an Argentine submarine and the following morning the ship's Wessex, XP142 'Humphrey', was despatched and found the *Santa Fé* nine miles outside Grytviken harbour. The American-built submarine was leaving South Georgia after landing reinforcements.

The Wessex dropped two depth charges which

straddled the *Santa Fé*, seriously damaging the submarine and forcing her to surface. 'Humphrey' then called up three Wasps, one from HMS *Plymouth* and two from the ice patrol ship HMS *Endurance* (including XS527, the first production aircraft). Their Nord AS12 wire-guided missiles punched holes through the thin skin of the conning tower. The *Santa Fé* limped into Grytviken harbour and was out of the war. Later that day 'Humphrey' and the Wasps from *Plymouth* and *Endurance* were in action again, this time spotting for the naval bombardment of Argentine positions before Marines and SAS men retook the island.

No 829 Squadron, which shares the Royal Naval Air Station at Portland with Nos 702 and 815 (Lynx) and 772 (Wessex) Squadrons, has two basic commitments:

(1): Small Ships' Flights. The provision of torpedo and missile-armed helicopters and personnel to frigates and survey ships such as HMS *Endurance*.

(2): Training. The training of new aircrew and maintenance personnel for all Wasp Flights.

In 1985, No 829 Squadron had 32 Wasps on strength, plus three non-flying airframes for ground instruction. There were 14 HQ aircraft, 10 used for flying training and four front-line reserve aircraft held at near-instant readiness. In addition, 17 aircraft equipped 16 Small Ships' Flights (*Endurance* having two aircraft).

Each Wasp ship's Flight has one aircraft, one pilot, a senior maintenance rating and five other maintainers. Morale throughout the Squadron, both on shore and at sea, is extremely high for several reasons. Firstly, pilots and senior maintenance ratings are given far more responsibility for their rank and position than on any other Fleet Air Arm squadron. Secondly, Wasp spares are in abundance as the type is steadily run down. This means that aircraft are rarely snagged for long periods as replacement equipment is nearly always readily at hand.

According to 829's Air Engineering Officer, Lt Cdr Dennis Bailie, the Wasp has proved to be robust and reliable with a serviceability rate exceeding 70%. He says: 'The simplicity of the Wasp, coupled with the reliability of the Nimbus engine, is reflected in the high serviceability. Stringent checks for corrosion and extensive anti-corrosion procedures have also ensured a long life for the Wasps'.

The size of the Wasp (its overall length is just 40ft 4in with rotors turning) does not mean that

Right:
A flight of Wasps from Portland overflying HMS *Dido*.
Roger Wasley

ROYAL NAVY
ROYAL NAVY
F104

MARINHA

AH-12A
KON. MARINE
236
236

SOUTHLAND
RNZN
NZ3905

it is simple to fly. From a pilot's point of view, the little Wasp has proved to be quite a handful and only above-average pilots are posted to No 829 Squadron. As one senior pilot explained: 'The Wasp tests you to your limits and it does sting back if you are not careful. It certainly teaches you airmanship'.

Pilot training courses at Portland last 22 weeks during which time students complete about 95 flying hours, involving up to 35 hours advanced flying training and the remainder geared to operational requirements. The second phase involves weaponry, launching torpedoes and firing missiles, and learning the tricky techniques of deck landing. Alighting on the restricted deck of a ship for the first time is without doubt the peak of the training syllabus. Some 20 deck landings are completed during the training period and many of them will be at night. On completion of his training, the pilot will go to sea as a Flight Commander.

The number of Wasps in Royal Navy service is steadily decreasing as the type is withdrawn and the larger twin-engined Westland Lynx increasingly takes over responsibility for anti-submarine and anti-surface vessel tasks. But Wasps have also seen extensive service with the naval air arms of Brazil, Indonesia, the Netherlands, New Zealand and South Africa. Former Royal Navy aircraft are continuing to be exported, ensuring the little Wasp with the sting in its tail will be flying for some years to come.

Left:
Another overseas customer was the Brazilian Navy.
Westland Aircraft

Below left:
The Royal Netherlands Navy was an early customer for the Wasp, designating it the AH-12A in service.
Bristol Siddeley Engines

Bottom left:
The Royal New Zealand Navy was still receiving ex-RN Wasps in 1985. NZ3905 was operating from RNZNS *Southland* when it visited Portland. *Peter R. March*

Below:
A quartet of Wasps flies over Portland Bill in salute to 21 years of service in 1984. *HMS Osprey*

David Oliver

Belize's Hash Busters

In 1638 a British ship foundered on a barrier reef off the western edge of the Caribbean Sea and its crew struggled ashore on a stretch of coast south of Mexico, to form an isolated settlement in central America. It was to become a haven for pirates during the 17th century, but by 1862 the strip of land, measuring 150 miles north to south and 68 miles east to west, was formally created a British Colony, despite objections from its neighbours, Mexico and Guatemala, to be named British Honduras.

Guatemala's claims to the territory have proved to be the more persistent and since the end of World War 2, the neighbour has threatened to invade on at least four occasions. Each time Guatemalan troops massed on the border, Britain had to rush warships and troops to reinforce the Garrison. In 1981, the country, now known as Belize, gained its independence, but requested that the British Garrison remain until the threat of an invasion by Guatemala had receded.

The present strength of the British Garrison is some 1,800, which includes 300 RAF personnel to support the detachments of four Harrier GR3s, four Puma HC1s, a Rapier Flight and a tactical air traffic control radar unit. In 1982, an Air Wing of the newly-formed Belize Defence Force was established at Belize's International Airport. Commanded by Sqn Ldr Dick Woodhead, who is on loan from the RAF as is his No 2, Flt Lt Dave Harris, the 12-man unit is equipped with two Pilatus BN-2B Defender

Below:
A BDF Defender, fitted with machine gun pods, refuelling at the Air Wing base at Belize International Airport.
All photographs David Oliver

Right:
An RAF Puma of 1563 Flight over the jungle of Belize. They are used to fly marijuana-burning BDF troops to the fields.

Below right:
A BDF Defender at Punta Gorda, the largest town in the south of Belize.

aircraft that were given to Belize by the British Government in 1983. Named *Tapir* and *Toucan* after the national animal and bird of Belize, the aircraft are equipped with HF radio, Skyshout aerial loudspeaker system, Loran C navigation system, twin 7.62mm machine gun pods, and one of them has Bendix weather radar. While the immediate threat of a Guatemalan invasion has temporarily receded, although if the present offshore oil explorations should prove to be positive or the British should decide to pull out of Belize, it may return, the main threat to the country's stability is undoubtedly the drug trade.

Since the early 1980s when it was discovered that Belizean marijuana was of a better quality than that grown in the biggest producer in the western hemisphere, Columbia, farmers have been forsaking the traditional crops of maize, rice and bananas, for the easier to grow and far more lucrative drug. Now that Belize has achieved the dubious distinction of becoming the second biggest marijuana producer in the western hemisphere, the drug trade is occupying more and more of the Belize Defence Force's time and resources, with the Air Wing in the forefront of the fight against the growers and the smugglers.

While the BDF relies on its own intelligence and occasional informers, who are usually legitimate farmers who have missed out on the drug trade for one reason or another, aerial

surveillance is proving to be most effective. As information about the illegal crops can be very slow in reaching the authorities on the ground, (things move very slowly in Belize, where there are few passable roads and even fewer working telephones) the BDF Defenders make regular patrols over the likely growing areas where freshly-cleared jungle in remote places is easy to spot from the air. The fields, which may be from one to 50 acres in size, once spotted, are left until the crop is almost ready for harvesting while the surrounding area will searched for any tree-felling activity which may signify the start of an illegal airstrip. If none is found, the fields are burned. In 1984 some 1,500 fields containing 4 million marijuana plants were destroyed by the BDF as a result of aerial surveys. Again, due to the lack of usable roads in the country, it is difficult to move troops quickly overland, so when a field is to be burned, elements of the BDF and Belize Police are flown to the area by RAF Pumas under the guidance of a Defender which acts as an aerial command post during the operation. If an illegal airstrip is in the vicinity, the troops will hide in the surrounding jungle and hope to arrest the smuggler and aircraft.

Aerial drug smuggling has developed into a sophisticated industry during the last 10 years. Centred on the southern states of the USA, many experienced pilots, a lot of them Vietnam veterans, have found a lucrative, and exciting way of making a living where the rewards now exceed the risks involved. This was not always the case. When time-expired commercial and ex-military aircraft were used it was a precarious occupation with more than 100 aged drug-smuggler aircraft crashes recorded in 1980. Although the DC-3 and Beechcraft 18 remain two of the most popular types in use, in a list of types ranging from ex-Belgian Air Force Pembrokes to Learjets, most of the aircraft used now are modern, reliable, high performance, light twins built by Cessna, Piper and Beech. Of the estimated 150 flights a day into the US, at least one will have come from Belize, which is only 750 miles from Florida or Texas.

Left:
Two BDF Air Wain Defenders patrol over one of the many coral islands on the barrier reef of Belize.

Right:
One of the few straight roads in Belize, the Western Highway, is used as an illegal airstrip by drug smugglers.

Below:
Four US-registered aircraft arrested on illegal airstrips by the BDF seen at Belize International where they will be sold by the Government.

Above:
Two arrested aircraft, a Piper Navajo and a Cessna 404.

Left:
A bullet hole in a Queen Air that had been 'shot down' by the BDF.

Above right:
An arrested Beech 18 at Belize International.

Right:
A Cessna in the Caribbean Sea off the coast of Belize, having run out of fuel within yards of the barrier reef, on an illegal flight.

On a number of occasions, illegal aircraft have been picked up by the RAF radar, but more often than not they have been spotted by the Defenders on a recce over the illegal airstrips. If possible, Sqn Ldr Woodhead will land to try to prevent the smuggler from taking off, but if it appears that it is about to leave before this can be done, the ground forces will move in to prevent its escape. It was at such a time that the BDF shot down their first aircraft when they opened fire on a Beech Queen Air as it attempted to take off. The troops came out of their jungle hiding place with guns blazing and although the aircraft was hit a number of times, it was the pilot putting his hands over his face to protect himself, thus releasing the controls, that caused the aircraft to run off the runway and come to rest in the surrounding maize field with damage to the undercarriage, wing tip and propeller. During the last few years, the BDF has arrested 10 aircraft, all US-registered, including two Cessna 210s, two Piper Aztecs, a Pilatus Porter, a Beech 18, Twin Bonanza and Queen Air, and two Cessna 404s, one of which

N569

Above:
Another of the many US-registered aircraft 'rotting' in Belize after seizure.

became the Air Wing's first aircraft prior to the delivery of its Defenders. Whenever possible, Dick Woodhead or Dave Harris fly the impounded aircraft out of the airstrip to Belize International. There the aircraft await the outcome of the court case before being sold by the Belize Government. One such flight nearly ended in disaster when one engine of a captured Beechcraft 18 failed while being ferried back to Belize, but having touched down safely, Sqn Ldr Woodhead again nearly came to grief by running off the runway when the tail-wheel locked.

Few of the pilots have been arrested, as they, along with the suppliers disappear into the jungle at the first sign of trouble. Typical of those who have been caught was David Wright, a 30-year old American, who had 2,000lb of marijuana aboard his aircraft. This one load would fetch $1½ million on the streets in the USA. Despite his bail being set at $100,000, Wright skipped the country before his trial came to court and was probably back in business a few days later.

All that the authorities can do is to plough up the illegal runways, many of which are large enough to take a DC-3, keep the bail money and sell the aircraft for what they can get. The government has tried to deter the smugglers by restricting the sale of aviation fuel to only two airports, Belize Municipal and International, but most of the aircraft involved are fitted with extra tanks to enable them to make the round trip to the States without re-fuelling. Meanwhile, the overworked, and underfinanced, Air Wing has had maritime surveillance added to its growing list of roles. With place names such as Condemned Point, Gallon Jug and Crows Nest Cay harping back to the days when pirates sailed the waters of Belize, the BDF is attempting to keep a check on their 20th century successors, the drug-smugglers. The Air Wing working in conjunction with the newly created Maritime Wing of the BDF, which is equipped with two British-built Wasp patrol boats, watch the many, and often uninhabited, coral islands that lie along the barrier reef some 10 miles off the coast of Belize. The islands, or cays, provide an ideal haven for the drug trade ships that sail across the Caribbean to the Bahamas or the States. Some of the islands even have their own airstrips — for the use of wealthy American tourists!

It is clear that while the demand for marijuana in the USA persists, the drug trade in Belize will continue to flourish, as a large percentage of the country's 140,000 inhabitants are involved in it. The need is for a greater amount of that Government's limited resources to be used in the fight, and for more money to be put into an expanded BDF Air Wing in particular.

WIN A WEEKEND FOR TWO IN THE RAINBOW HOTEL OF YOUR CHOICE

IAL ANNUAL COMPETITION

Are you a real aviation enthusiast? Can you recognise any type of aircraft likely to be seen flying over Britain today? Do you know your QFE from your QDM, a C-12 from a C-21 or why Aresti gets into the cockpit of many aerobatic light aircraft? Put yourself to the test with this two part brain-teasing quiz. Simply read the rules below, fill in the official entry form and send it and the competition voucher (to be found at the front of the Annual) to IAN ALLAN LTD. In the event of a tie, the winners will be chosen by means of a draw.

PRIZES

- FIRST PRIZE (One winner)
  A WEEKEND FOR TWO *at half board in the Rainbow Hotel of your choice.*
- SECOND PRIZE (One winner)
  A DAY OUT AT RAF CONINGSBY *— see Phantoms, Tornados and the Battle of Britain Memorial Flight from the runway.*
- THIRD PRIZE (Five winners)
  A TWO-YEAR SUBSCRIPTION *to the Ian Allan Ltd magazine of your choice.*

RULES

1. Entries must be made on the official entry form published in *Aircraft Illustrated* and *Armed Forces* in the August 1986, December 1986 and February 1987 issues and in *Air Extra* 56 and 57.
2. All entries must be accompanied by a competition voucher from *Aircraft Illustrated Annual 1987*.
3. The judges' decision will be final.
4. No correspondence regarding this competition can be entered into.
5. No employee or his/her family of the Ian Allan Group of companies may enter this competition.
6. The closing date for this competition is 28 February 1987. Entries received after this date will not be accepted.
7. Prizewinners will be notified by post; all will also be announced in the May-dated issues of *Aircraft Illustrated, Armed Forces* and *Air Extra*.

Part 1

First of all can you recognise these 25 aircraft? You must give full details for each photo, including manufacturer, name and any designation.

1

2

3

4

5

6

7

8

9

10

11

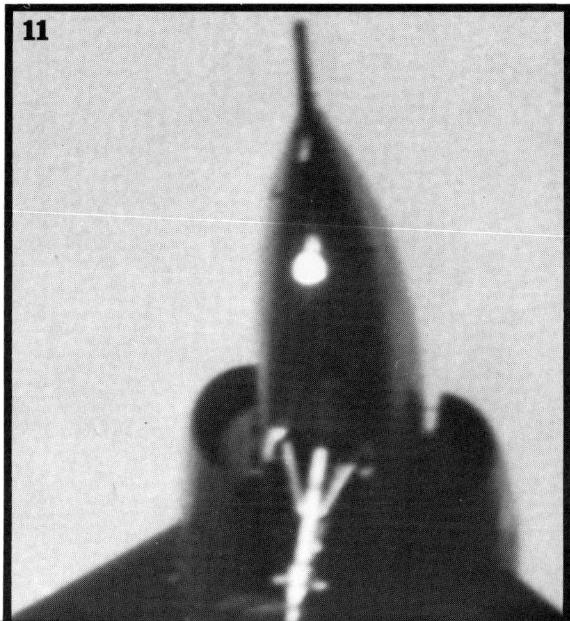

12

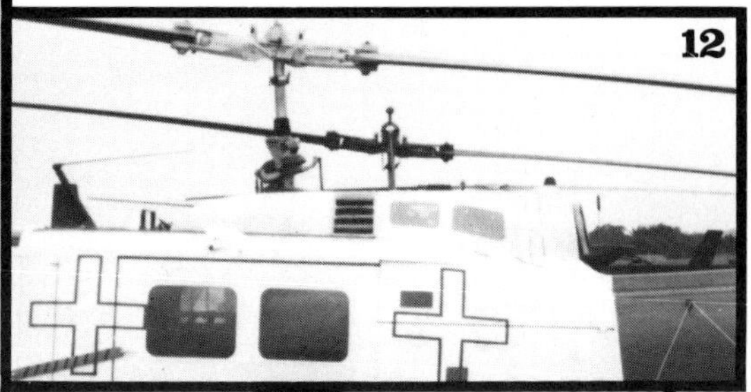

13

14

15

16

17

18

19

20

21

22

23

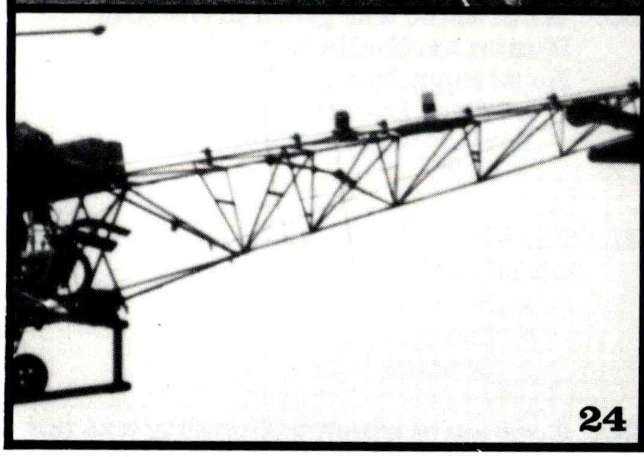
24

25

Part 2

Now have a go at this Aero-Quiz. Multi-choice possible answers are provided, but in two cases none of the three optional answers is correct. Give your answers a, b, or c if you think one of the possibilities is correct; otherwise put x if you think that none of them is the right answer. In the space at the end put the numbers and correct answers to these two questions.

1. **What was the name of the top scoring British ace in World War 1?**
   a Edward Mannock
   b Albert Ball
   c James McCudden

2. **In which country is the airline Busy Bee based?**
   a Norway
   b United States
   c Netherlands

3. **Approximately how many British operated aircraft were lost in World War 2?**
   a 25,000
   b 35,000
   c 45,000

4. **What is the NATO code name for the Sukhoi Su-27?**
   a Foxtrot
   b Flanker
   c Flounder

5. **When did the SEPECAT Jaguar first fly?**
   a 1968
   b 1970
   c 1972

6. **Which aircraft was produced in the greatest numbers between 1939 and 1945?**
   a Spitfire
   b Messerschmitt 109
   c Ilyushin Il-2

7. **What aircraft type scored the last British air combat victory of World War 2?**
   a Corsair
   b Spitfire
   c Seafire

8. **What type of American light aircraft has been produced in the largest numbers since 1945?**
   a Cessna 172
   b Piper Cub
   c Piper Cherokee